# BeagleBone Media Center

A practical guide to transforming your BeagleBone into a fully functional media center

**David Lewin**

PUBLISHING

BIRMINGHAM - MUMBAI

# BeagleBone Media Center

Copyright © 2015 Packt Publishing

First published: January 2015

Production reference: 1220115

Published by Packt Publishing Ltd.
Livery Place
35 Livery Street
Birmingham B3 2PB, UK.

ISBN 978-1-78439-999-3

www.packtpub.com

# Credits

**Author**
David Lewin

**Reviewers**
Eric Feuilleaubois

Naoya Hashimoto

Pei JIA

Chidananda Matada
Shivananda

**Commissioning Editor**
Amarabha Banerjee

**Acquisition Editor**
Larissa Pinto

**Content Development Editor**
Neeshma Ramakrishnan

**Technical Editor**
Faisal Siddiqui

**Copy Editors**
Dipti Kapadia

Rashmi Sawant

**Project Coordinator**
Danuta Jones

**Proofreaders**
Ameesha Green

Lawrence A. Herman

**Indexer**
Hemangini Bari

**Production Coordinator**
Manu Joseph

**Cover Work**
Manu Joseph

# About the Author

**David Lewin** was introduced early to electronics and computers by TRS-80, Atari, and Commodore 64; he has never quit since then. He spends his free time watching out for technology for the next generation of embedded systems when he is not exploring philosophy.

David is a passionate and creative embedded developer who spent 20 years working for automotive companies such as Renault, Peugeot, and Faurecia, as well as for satellites with Thales Alenia Space. He currently works in Sophia Antipolis, the French Riviera Silicon Valley, designing industrial embedded systems.

A book is a real personal investment, and I'd like to thank Lisa for her patience, support, and advice. Thanks to my parents for supporting me in my early days; it is also thanks to them that I found the way to write to this book. Thanks toSarah and Lisa as well. Thanks to Eric and Carol for their time and efforts. I'd like also to thank Neeshma and Larissa at Packt Publishing for their precious help. Besides, I'd also like to thank the open source community as they allow you to benefit from the BeagleBone hardware and software.

I would also like to thank Naoya, Rachel, and Jason (the syntaxic killer) for their great work as I really appreciate what they brought to the book.

# About the Reviewers

**Naoya Hashimoto** has been working on system design and integration with open source software for years. In the past few years, his career and interests have been shifting toward cloud engineering mainly for AWS with orchestration tools such as Chef or CloudFormation.

He has reviewed *Icinga Network Monitoring*, *Home Security System with BeagleBone*, and *Building networks and servers using BeagleBone*, both by Packt Publishing:

> Thanks to the author and project coordinator Danuta, who gave me this opportunity to review the book. I am very impressed with her work and this project because we can create a media center device with BeagleBone and open source software. I hope that we get more such opportunities to work with BeagleBone and other open source software.

**Pei JIA** holds a PhD degree in computer science from the University of Essex, with full financial aid by Overseas Research Studentship (ORS). He specializes in various computer vision algorithms (particularly, 2D and 3D morphable models) and has extensive embedded machine vision experience. He is the pioneer of advocating all kinds of open source, both software and hardware. He has just designed his own smart house in beautiful British Columbia using a BeagleBone Black-based control center. Recently, he launched his enterprise, Longer Vision Tech., in ShenZhen, China, which focuses on designing intelligent vision systems. He has been keeping a close eye on the electronics market and a cooperating closely with the connections with in Seattle and Silicon Valley.

It is my pleasure to be invited to review this book, *BeagleBone Media Center*, whose title attracted me at first sight. Various single-board computers (SBC) have now emerged, such as BeagleBone Black, Raspberry Pi, Banana Pi Pro, and so on. It's certain that BeagleBone Black has been playing an important role in the development of SBCs. This book elaborates on how to design a media center based on a BeagleBone Black SBC and it comes down to some open source software, such as MediaDrop. I strongly suggest that you read this book (in particular, open source advocators).

**Chidananda Matada Shivananda** is an electrical engineering graduate who specializes in system dynamics and controls at Villanova University. He has 2 years of industry experience that involves automotive engine management software development at Robert Bosch, India. His interests lie in embedded systems, mobile robotics, and control systems.

I would like to thank Packt Publishing for giving me this wonderful opportunity.

# www.PacktPub.com

## Support files, eBooks, discount offers, and more

For support files and downloads related to your book, please visit www.PacktPub.com.

Did you know that Packt offers eBook versions of every book published, with PDF and ePub files available? You can upgrade to the eBook version at www.PacktPub.com and as a print book customer, you are entitled to a discount on the eBook copy. Get in touch with us at service@packtpub.com for more details.

At www.PacktPub.com, you can also read a collection of free technical articles, sign up for a range of free newsletters and receive exclusive discounts and offers on Packt books and eBooks.

https://www2.packtpub.com/books/subscription/packtlib

Do you need instant solutions to your IT questions? PacktLib is Packt's online digital book library. Here, you can search, access, and read Packt's entire library of books.

## Why subscribe?

- Fully searchable across every book published by Packt
- Copy and paste, print, and bookmark content
- On demand and accessible via a web browser

## Free access for Packt account holders

If you have an account with Packt at www.PacktPub.com, you can use this to access PacktLib today and view 9 entirely free books. Simply use your login credentials for immediate access.

# Table of Contents

# Preface

The still young market of embedded boards is growing each day, owing to the Raspberry Pi effect. These single-board computers help you solve common problems, such as analyzing a network, programming without a PC, and others. The BeagleBone Black has all of these features, but at the same time, you can broaden your horizons to perform interesting tasks using the expansion capability of the board. Whether you use the basic version of the board or improve it with different accessories available in the market, this board will come in handy to help you decide and create the various tasks you want to perform with it. This book is designed to provide you with the knowledge to explore the world of BeagleBone Black.

Welcome aboard!

## What this book covers

*Chapter 1*, *Transforming Your BeagleBone Black into a Media Server*, begins with an introduction to help you better understand why it is in your interest to have your own personal server. This chapter then describes the steps required for the installation of an improved multimedia server on steroids.

*Chapter 2*, *Media Management, Shares, and Social Activities*, gives indications to use your new server in a connected world. It begins with an explanation of the workflow that needs to be followed; there are also indications to understand what an administrator should do. The chapter ends with social sharing to let you share your contents with your friends or members of your family.

*Chapter 3, Examples of Real-world Situations*, deals with security because a connected server also needs to safely manage your publications. This chapter introduces you to the security role followed by two scenarios based on real-life experiences: one for a house, and another for professional activities.

*Chapter 4, Getting Your Own Video and Feeds*, discusses how to improve the existing server by giving you the opportunity to provide your own personal video streams. This chapter gives you the keys for hardware detection. It also presents a different topic that is still based on multimedia: configuring the server for RSS feeds.

*Chapter 5, Building Your Media Player*, describes the real USP of the BeagleBone Black: capes. Thus, it gives you a way to extend your board in order to create funnier and useful projects. In addition, with this exciting chapter, you will be able to build a device that can display movies and play music without making your imagination compromise because you can also extend this extension board through connectors and additional networks.

*Chapter 6, Illuminate Your Imagination with Your Own Projects*, lets you enter into the software part of the book using "Matrix Revolution," a fun project with funny tools: you'll use the 8 x 8 bicolor LEDs matrix from Adafruit connected to the BeagleBone Black. After a good introduction to the hardware of the board, the remaining part of this chapter is then split into three examples, starting with a simple example that allows beginners to start smoothly in Python and understand the main programming concepts related to a server and a client. This is followed by an improved version of the first example with a GUI as a laboratory for your experiments. It finally ends with a totally different example written in C++, which is a pattern generator, so you'll be able to display every disco pattern you like.

*Appendix A, Troubleshooting and Tricks to Improve Your Server*, covers the topics that will help you resolve issues that you might face while working with your servers, including some useful tools and troubleshooting steps.

*Appendix B, Ideas to Improve Your Server*, introduces some ideas to improve your server functionality.

# What you need for this book

To run the book's examples, you will need a running Python environment, including the virtualenv package. The source code will be available from the dedicated GitHub repository and website as well. In all cases, *Chapter 5, Building Your Media Player*, and *Chapter 6, Illuminate Your Imagination with Your Own Projects*, will discuss how to install, compile, and run the examples.

# Who this book is for

This book is intended for those who want to overcome the limitations of standard projects by learning electronics and programming and by using their imagination, knowledge, and passion.

# Conventions

In this book, you will find a number of styles of text that distinguish between different kinds of information. Here are some examples of these styles and an explanation of their meaning.

Code words in text, database table names, folder names, filenames, file extensions, pathnames, dummy URLs, user input, and Twitter handles are shown as follows: "We can include other contexts through the use of the `include` directive."

A block of code is set as follows:

```
grid = ColorEightByEight(address=0x70)
```

Any command-line input or output is written as follows:

```
debian@arm:~$ Install v4l-utils
```

**New terms** and **important words** are shown in bold. Words that you see on the screen, in menus or dialog boxes for example, appear in the text like this: "Clicking the **Next** button moves you to the next screen."

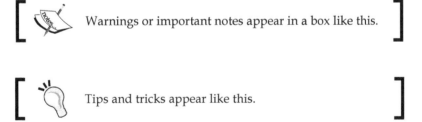

Warnings or important notes appear in a box like this.

Tips and tricks appear like this.

# Reader feedback

Feedback from our readers is always welcome. Let us know what you think about this book—what you liked or may have disliked. Reader feedback is important for us to develop titles that you really get the most out of.

To send us general feedback, simply send an e-mail to feedback@packtpub.com, and mention the book title via the subject of your message.

If there is a topic that you have expertise in and you are interested in either writing or contributing to a book, see our author guide on www.packtpub.com/authors.

# Customer support

Now that you are the proud owner of a Packt book, we have a number of things to help you to get the most from your purchase.

# Errata

Although we have taken every care to ensure the accuracy of our content, mistakes do happen. If you find a mistake in one of our books—maybe a mistake in the text or the code—we would be grateful if you would report this to us. By doing so, you can save other readers from frustration and help us improve subsequent versions of this book. If you find any errata, please report them by visiting http://www.packtpub.com/submit-errata, selecting your book, clicking on the **errata submission form** link, and entering the details of your errata. Once your errata are verified, your submission will be accepted and the errata will be uploaded on our website, or added to any list of existing errata, under the Errata section of that title. Any existing errata can be viewed by selecting your title from http://www.packtpub.com/support.

# Piracy

Piracy of copyright material on the Internet is an ongoing problem across all media. At Packt, we take the protection of our copyright and licenses very seriously. If you come across any illegal copies of our works, in any form, on the Internet, please provide us with the location address or website name immediately so that we can pursue a remedy.

Please contact us at copyright@packtpub.com with a link to the suspected pirated material.

We appreciate your help in protecting our authors, and our ability to bring you valuable content.

## Questions

You can contact us at questions@packtpub.com if you are having a problem with any aspect of the book, and we will do our best to address it.

# 1
# Transforming Your BeagleBone Black into a Media Server

Sharing files, watching movies, listening to music, and all the other media-related activities are abundantly proposed as Internet services. Any provider can propose an MP3 aside books and eggs; you have to choose among subscriptions that most of the time include items that you don't need or never use. The chapters in this book won't discuss these online services that, if you do the math, cost you a lot, including questioning your privacy, of course. Instead, you are going to be like these providers, and the best one too. Why the best? Because you are the person who is best placed to know what you need. Indeed, as you will know how to implement the services that please you, you'll have the functionalities that will suit you the most.

## The choice that is not yours

I'm sure you'll prefer to select the applications you'll like to have at home instead of choosing among the fee subscriptions that providers impose on you.

Let's use an example: if you subscribe to *Netflix* or *Spotify*, you pay for the music or video titles you choose among their catalogs. It is obvious that these on-demand content providers offer an impressive choice, but this implies the following two major drawbacks.

# You'll still be restricted by their proposals

As royalties to the majors are required, any media content supplier is forced to constantly pay the titles it offers. This is the reason why:

- You might not be able to find a song
- You might find a studio recorded version although you wanted the live version
- Your music/movies selections might be removed from your playlist because the legal rights have changed

# You hardly manage your own content

Although the ability to add personal files has been added recently, there are a few limitations, as follows:

- You cannot perform a search in these topics or restrict a search to your collection
- It also lacks a ranking by genre or composer, for enthusiasts of classical and film music
- Artists' profiles still do not distinguish between studio albums, concerts, and compilations

# Your server, your rules

The solution that we are going to implement is based on different software, according to our choices. I mean real choices. Quoting Wikipedia, a server can be defined as follows:

> A **server** *is a running instance of an application (*software*) capable of accepting requests from the client and giving responses accordingly. Servers can run on any computer including dedicated computers, which individually are also often referred to as "the server."*

# Powerful and straightforward software installations

That being said, you want a media server but you are not comfortable with these technologies, which might scare you or put you off. The applications used in this book are really straightforward to install and use; particularly, open source applications have been selected.

# Using dedicated hardware

Additionally, we are going to use an embedded board instead of the heavy, large, and power-consuming PCs so that we can also drastically reduce the costs. While we will focus on *BeagleBone Black* in this book, the chapters have been written to use most of the boards available on the market, such as Raspberry Pi, WandBoard, CubieBoard, and some others, as long as the board supports Linux and has a network connection.

The main goal of this approach is that you learn to be independent enough so that the next time you receive a promotional e-mail with music streaming advertising, you'll throw it away, smiling proudly.

This chapter is about installing a MediaDrop server, which will be introduced shortly. As promised, it will be quite easy (really easy, in fact); no compilation or library will be invoked. Before the installation process itself, we will have a quick look at some situations that an embedded board is able to resolve. We will also find out why we should consider a server philosophy instead of a traditional computer. This will impact the remaining part of the book because the board will be accessed through an SSH connection; we will also have to take into consideration our available free space to store our applications and media contents. Then, we will start the installation part for the MediaDrop server itself. Management and security tasks have been split in additional chapters, so you can skip them and get back later if you want.

Welcome to the first step of your independence.

In this chapter, we will talk about the following topics:

- Looking at daily scenarios for media usage
- Down to the cave is a server without a head — headless servers
- Preparing BeagleBone to be a server
- Let's get acquainted with our friend – MediaDrop
- MediaDrop installation steps
- Testing time – "Hello Server"
- Switching from development to production
- Let's take a walk in our new MediaDrop server

# Looking at daily scenarios for media usage

With some examples being more explicit than others, here's a sample of the situations you might already face or will face soon. Such a platform as MediaDrop can resolve them by nature:

- You have been requested to build a media system that is able to display a presentation video clip of a product you intend to promote (in a market, company, and so on). *A BeagleBone board with remote management will be handy, most of all if you have a lot of videos to handle.*

- From the precedent point, *compare the different PC and BeagleBone budgets.*

- Your wife asked you to watch the latest TV show episode from Netflix, but she doesn't want to use any computer for it. *Really?*

- As an employee, you want to improve yourself. Having access to e-learning would be a good thing. Does the local proxy server grant you access to such media-related things? *A local device having access to local contents is so easy to deploy for each desktop.*

- A company wants its employees to use internal communication — *easy and fast as podcasts by using the boards on the local network*

# Down in the cave is a server without a head – headless servers

Behind such a strange title are the motivations for the server that you will optimize needing to be headless. Even though BeagleBone is able to display GUIs, shiny graphics, and desktops, you need to get used to interacting with your server *as if you are in a cave with limited light* and no eye-candy gadgets. Here are some of the reasons why:

- **Resources**: The most important reason is that a graphical desktop consumes the most amount of resources. Consider not only the GUI resources but also the graphical server it relies on; therefore, it needs more CPU, memory, and disk space.

- **Space**: Our server can be physically anywhere. Thanks to its reduced dimensions, it is easy to put BeagleBone in a place and forget about it. This can be next to the desktop, behind your monitor, in a cupboard, and in your car as well.

- **Access and simplicity**: If you need to get access to a server or maybe several servers, you will really not want to bother connecting to each dedicated server. If you need to administer 11 desktops, this will require you to connect to each one. On the other hand, by using a console environment, you are ensured having the same behaviors each time.

 Wait a minute! Just by taking a look back at the title and after all that has been said, the Addams Family might have used a BeagleBone server.

Among others, these reasons justify the time that you are going to spend on your experiments. It's worth it.

# Preparing BeagleBone to be a server

As mentioned previously, we will use the **BeagleBone Black** embedded board for our experiments. It is assumed that you will have completed the following:

- After visiting the **Getting Started** page (http://beagleboard.org/getting-started) and executing all the mentioned steps, the board will be just started and you will be connected to it. All through the book, the PuTTY program was used for this.

- The board is using the current official bone-debian-7.5-2014-05-14-2gb, which is related to a 2 GB SD card (as shown in the next screenshot). Nevertheless, it's strongly advised that you use cards with a larger size and we'll soon see why.

- Your board is identified in your local network; when required, we'll use the address 192.168.0.15, which you will need to adapt according to your local network. Most of the rooters provide a web interface for this purpose.

- The default credentials are debian as the username and temppwd as the password.

# Booting from an SD Card or flash (eMMC)

BeagleBone Black has the advantage of booting either from an SD card or on-board flash (eMMC). The pros and cons of each of these is beyond the scope of this chapter. Generally, for this book, you should rely on the SD card support for the following reasons:

- **You can use all the space you want without sacrificing any other partition**: On flash, you are limited to the provided space, which is again limited by design.

- **You can change your mind whenever you want**: If you want to install all the applications described in this book, you can either use different SD cards or buy a bigger one.

- **It is an error-proof solution**: If you have never burnt any electronic device or broken the code, you should. Of course, not intentionally but because you pushed the limits. Many inventions have been found by accident, such as Penicillin, Teflon, and even Brownies and Tatin tart. So, if sometimes you are not able to boot the system, you will always have the possibility to get back to the situation you started with, using the SD card, by writing a new image to it.

 Here's a reminder: in order to boot to the SD card, just power on the board and keep pressing the "user button," the one near the SD card.

The SD card induces small additional latencies that you won't even notice, so it is better to use it as a sandbox. So feel free to explore and try crazy things so that you can learn without limitations and worry.

# Extending the root limitations on a fresh installation

If you update or install anything right away after a boot, you will encounter problems related to disk space.

Indeed, if you use PuTTY (www.putty.org) or any other SSH software to connect yourself to the board (such as, 192.168.0.15) and look at the rootfs space information, you can guess that the available size will be quickly saturated.

```
debian@beaglebone:~$ uname -a
Linux beaglebone 3.8.13-bone50 #1 SMP Tue May 13 13:24:52 UTC 2014 armv71 GNU/Linux
debian@beaglebone:~$ df -h
Filesystem       Size  Used Avail Use% Mounted on
rootfs           1.6G  1.5G  1.6M 100% /
udev             10M      0   10M   0% /dev
tmpfs           100M   664K   99M   1% /run
/dev/mmcblk0p2   1.6G  1.5G  1.6M 100% /
tmpfs           249M      0  249M   0% /dev/shm
tmpfs           249M      0  249M   0% /sys/fs/cgroup
tmpfs           5.0M      0  5.0M   0% /run/lock
tmpfs           100M      0  100M   0% /run/user
/dev/mmcblk0p1   96M    70M   27M  73% /boot/uboot
/dev/mmcblk1p2   1.7G   863M  727M  55% /media/rootfs
/dev/mmcblk1p1   96M    72M   25M  75% /media/boot
```

The SD card has little space left the first time

So, as the server administrator, it is up to you to resolve the size constraints.

 Like everyone else, you might want to use an SD card with a bigger size. This will produce exactly the same result as in the preceding figure, as you will use the same partition scheme.

The next topic will describe how you can achieve this task easily.

# Extending your root's partition

The default free space is really small; for example, you can fill it completely with just one upgrade. As a result, the very first thing to do at boot is to resize the /root partition.

Resizing a partition is not recommended for first timers. The good news is that you won't have to enter many commands; you can make your life easy by relying on a dedicated script provided with the board, which will do all that for you.

Enter the following two commands:

```
debian@beaglebone:~$ cd /opt/scripts/tools/
debian@beaglebone:/opt/scripts/tools/$ git pull
```

```
debian@beaglebone:~$ cd /opt/scripts/tools/
debian@beaglebone:/opt/scripts/tools$ git pull
remote: Counting objects: 546, done.
remote: Compressing objects: 100% (176/176), done.
remote: Total 530 (delta 390), reused 488 (delta 349)
Receiving objects: 100% (530/530), 69.74 KiB, done.
Resolving deltas: 100% (390/390), completed with 9 local objects.
From https://github.com/RobertCNelson/boot-scripts
   8690159..c84610b  master       -> origin/master
Updating 8690159..c84610b
Fast-forward
 boot/am335x_evm.sh                                 |   52 ++--
 boot/omap3_beagle.sh                               |   32 +--
 boot/omap5_uevm.sh                                 |   54 ++++
 device/bone/capes/BB-BEAGLELOGIC/beaglelogic-pru0  | Bin 0 -> 11160 bytes
 device/bone/capes/BB-BEAGLELOGIC/beaglelogic-pru1  | Bin 0 -> 12648 bytes
 device/bone/capes/BBB_Audio_Cape_RevB/asound.state | 1311 +++++++++++++++++++++++++++++++++++++++++++++++++
 device/bone/tester/eeprom-u-boot.sh                |  277 ++++++++++++++++++++++
 tools/beaglebone-black-eMMC-flasher.sh             |  155 +++++++-----
 tools/eMMC/init-eMMC-flasher-v2.sh                 |  345 +++++++++++++++++++++++++
 tools/grow_partition.sh                            |   28 +--
 tools/init-eMMC-flasher.sh                         |  391 ++++++++++++++++++++++++++++
 tools/update_bootloader.sh                         |   27 +-
 tools/update_kernel.sh                             |  140 +++++++++--
 tools/wm/efl.sh                                    |  170 +++++++++++++
 tools/wm/lxqt.sh                                   |    1 +
 tools/wm/maynard.sh                                |  114 +++++++++
 tools/wm/weston-drm.sh                             |    7 +
 tools/wm/weston-fbdev.sh                           |    8 +
 tools/wm/weston.sh                                 |   12 +
 19 files changed, 2985 insertions(+), 139 deletions(-)
 create mode 100755 boot/omap5_uevm.sh
 create mode 100644 device/bone/capes/BB-BEAGLELOGIC/beaglelogic-pru0
 create mode 100644 device/bone/capes/BB-BEAGLELOGIC/beaglelogic-pru1
 create mode 100644 device/bone/capes/BBB_Audio_Cape_RevB/asound.state
 create mode 100755 device/bone/tester/eeprom-u-boot.sh
 create mode 100755 tools/eMMC/init-eMMC-flasher-v2.sh
 create mode 100755 tools/init-eMMC-flasher.sh
 create mode 100755 tools/wm/efl.sh
 create mode 100755 tools/wm/maynard.sh
 create mode 100755 tools/wm/weston-drm.sh
 create mode 100755 tools/wm/weston-fbdev.sh
 create mode 100755 tools/wm/weston.sh
debian@beaglebone:/opt/scripts/tools$ ls
beaglebone-black-eMMC-flasher.sh  eMMC      grow_partition.sh    start_cloud9.sh      update_initrd.sh  wm
developers                        graphics  init-eMMC-flasher.sh update_bootloader.sh update_kernel.sh
debian@beaglebone:/opt/scripts/tools$ ./grow_partition.sh
```

In this directory, we have downloaded the last code from the official repository, so we can start the script thereafter:

```
debian@beaglebone:/opt/scripts/tools/$ sudo ./grow_partition.sh
```

While running, this script will display a lot of details, which, thanks to the author, you don't have to care about.

```
debian@beaglebone:/opt/scripts/tools$ sudo ./grow_partition.sh
sfdisk: backing up partition layout.

Disk /dev/mmcblk0: 246240 cylinders, 4 heads, 16 sectors/track
Old situation:
Units = mebibytes of 1048576 bytes, blocks of 1024 bytes, counting from 0

   Device Boot Start    End    MiB    #blocks   Id  System
/dev/mmcblk0p1    *      1      96     96        98304    e  W95 FAT16 (LBA)
             start: (c,h,s) expected (32,0,1) found (0,32,33)
             end: (c,h,s) expected (1023,3,16) found (12,93,17)
/dev/mmcblk0p2          97     1699   1603      1641472   83  Linux
             start: (c,h,s) expected (1023,3,16) found (12,93,18)
             end: (c,h,s) expected (1023,3,16) found (216,183,31)
/dev/mmcblk0p3          0      -      0          0        0  Empty
/dev/mmcblk0p4          0      -      0          0        0  Empty
New situation:
Units = mebibytes of 1048576 bytes, blocks of 1024 bytes, counting from 0

   Device Boot Start    End    MiB    #blocks   Id  System
/dev/mmcblk0p1    *      1      96     96        98304    e  W95 FAT16 (LBA)
/dev/mmcblk0p2          97     7694   7598      7780352   83  Linux
/dev/mmcblk0p3          0      -      0          0        0  Empty
/dev/mmcblk0p4          0      -      0          0        0  Empty
Successfully wrote the new partition table

Re-reading the partition table ...
BLKRRPART: Device or resource busy
The command to re-read the partition table failed.
Run partprobe(8), kpartx(8) or reboot your system now,
before using mkfs
If you created or changed a DOS partition, /dev/foo7, say, then use dd(1)
to zero the first 512 bytes:  dd if=/dev/zero of=/dev/foo7 bs=512 count=1
(See fdisk(8).)
debian@beaglebone:/opt/scripts/tools$ 
```

These are the commands that you won't have to learn

You can now go on to reboot your board (don't forget to press the user's button), as follows:

```
debian@beaglebone:/opt/scripts/tools/$ sudo reboot
```

Now, if you check, you'll see that the free space has been resized to the SD card's capabilities.

```
debian@beaglebone:~$ df -h
Filesystem        Size  Used Avail Use% Mounted on
rootfs            7.3G  1.5G  5.6G  21% /
udev               10M     0   10M   0% /dev
tmpfs             100M  640K   99M   1% /run
/dev/mmcblk0p2    7.3G  1.5G  5.6G  21% /
tmpfs             249M     0  249M   0% /dev/shm
tmpfs             249M     0  249M   0% /sys/fs/cgroup
tmpfs             5.0M     0  5.0M   0% /run/lock
tmpfs             100M     0  100M   0% /run/user
/dev/mmcblk0p1     96M   70M   27M  73% /boot/uboot
/dev/mmcblk1p2    1.7G  863M  727M  55% /media/rootfs
/dev/mmcblk1p1     96M   72M   25M  75% /media/boot
debian@beaglebone:~$
```

An 8-GB resized SD card

Now, you can continue with the update and upgrade…

The local /root partition from the SD card is fast to implement and easy to use. Nevertheless, thinking about how you will organize your server is a good habit. Linux can handle multiple remote filesystems that you can write to. For instance, for all your media contents, you can use an NFS partition from a distant drive or a device that supports uPnP.

# Let's get acquainted with our friend – MediaDrop

Through this chapter, we'll talk about a great project called MediaDrop (http://mediadrop.net/), which lets you manage music, movies, and podcasts through a nice web interface.

Mediadrop has all the features that a media server can offer, as follows:

- HTML5 and Flash video
- A CMS-like interface available from a browser and mobile devices (iPhone and Android)
- Have as many users as you want, without any restrictions to access your content, unless you choose to have restrictions

- User management with many capabilities, such as comment editor, like buttons, tags, and so on

- Storage capability, which lets you choose where your file will be located

- An administration-dedicated interface with easy access

- Access roles capability

- Social media sharing (Twitter, Facebook, and so on) and video/audio links possibility

- It's open source, which means that you have access to the engine itself, you can improve it, or you can become a part of this community at `https://github.com/mediadrop/mediadrop`

- The Mediadrop platform can be extended through Python scripts

# MediaDrop installation steps

The following sections will take you through the installation of Mediadrop.

## BBB Debian – prerequisites

Now that your system is ready to accept all the applications you want to install, let's begin with the MySQL part:

```
debian@beaglebone:~$ install mysql-server mysql-client
```

 Actually, `sudo apt-get install` works behind the scenes. From this point onwards, we'll rely on aliases to ease our life from the command line. Refer to the *Appendix* to get all the details.

During this you'll be asked for the database's root password, then the remaining system files:

```
debian@beaglebone:~$ install libjpeg-dev zlib1g-dev libfreetype6-dev
libmysqlclient-dev python-dev
```

Finally, the Python-related requirements that will help you in virtual environments can be installed using the following command:

```
debian@beaglebone:~$ install python-setuptools python-virtualenv
```

With system requirements in place, you can set up MediaDrop in just six installation steps. Before doing that, you need to define a database for it.

# Setting up a dedicated database

You need to create some credentials and assign a user to a new MediaDrop database. It requires you to type only a few commands. If this is something that you don't want to do, the script is available on the GitHub companion website at https://github.com/dlewin/BeagleboneBlack-Server-Book.

Just execute the following command:

```
./create_mediadropdb.sh
```

Instead, if you are like me and want to control your entire system, then open a MySQL console, and pay attention to the syntax of the following command (with the ;):

```
debian@beaglebone:~$ mysql -u root -p
```

Then, fill in the password you have defined in the installation steps.

You will now have access to the MySQL console for all the database operations that MediaDrop requires. Now, perform the following steps:

1. Create your user with a password:

   ```
   create user 'debian'@'localhost'IDENTIFIED BY 'temppwd';
   ```

2. Create the MediaDrop database; pay attention to the use of capital letters:

   ```
   create database MediaDrop;
   ```

3. Now, we tell that we want to work on this database:

   ```
   use MediaDrop;
   ```

4. Set some rights on this database for the `debian` user:

```
grant create,insert,update,select,delete on MediaDrop.* to debian@
localhost;
```

```
exit
```

Here's a screenshot that shows these operations along with the related MySQL feedback you should get:

```
debian@beaglebone:~$ mysql -u root -p
Enter password:
Welcome to the MySQL monitor.  Commands end with ; or \g.
Your MySQL connection id is 40
Server version: 5.5.37-0+wheezy1 (Debian)

Copyright (c) 2000, 2014, Oracle and/or its affiliates. All rights reserved.

Oracle is a registered trademark of Oracle Corporation and/or its
affiliates. Other names may be trademarks of their respective
owners.

Type 'help;' or '\h' for help. Type '\c' to clear the current input statement.

mysql> create user 'debian'@'localhost' IDENTIFIED BY 'temppwd';
Query OK, 0 rows affected (0.00 sec)

mysql> create database MediaDrop;
Query OK, 1 row affected (0.00 sec)

mysql> use MediaDrop
Database changed
mysql> grant create,insert,update,select,delete on MediaDrop.* to debian@localhost;
Query OK, 0 rows affected (0.00 sec)

mysql> exit
Bye
debian@beaglebone:~$ 
```

# Step 1 – set up a Python virtual environment

MediaDrop has been programmed in Python, a simple but powerful language that we'll also use in *Chapter 6, Illuminate Your Imagination with Your Own Projects*. As plugins are also in Python, you are free to extend the platform as you wish.

Let's see how to define a dedicated environment for this purpose.

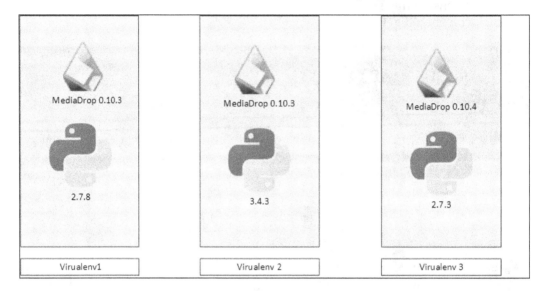

Virtual environments introduce a functionality provided with Python that I like to use: actually, with this functionality, you can resolve the problems of software versions and incompatibility. The principle is to use as many virtual spaces with different packages or executables as you want without any confusion that might create a broken system. Thanks to the isolation provided by this tool, you are guaranteed that it is kept as you want it to be and thus you always have a safe system.

> If you want to know more about **virtualenv**, take a look at https://
> virtualenv.readthedocs.org/en/latest/. There is also a
> **virtualenvwrapper** that is intended to ease the creation and deletion
> of many virtual environments at https://virtualenvwrapper.
> readthedocs.org/en/latest/.

Currently, we are using the 0.10.3 version of MediaDrop, but nothing stops you from trying the next version in order to test any side effects on your architecture. Thus, instead of executing the current environment, you'll just have to start MediaDrop from the *n+1* environment.

Virtual environment is presented just here, but you should create an environment each time you need different usages of an application or dependencies. It requires just less than a minute and can be done by performing the following steps:

1. Create the environment with a specific name; in our case, `venv`:

   ```
   debian@beaglebone:~$ virtualenv --distribute venv
   ```

2. Enter the dedicated virtual environment:

   ```
   debian@beaglebone:~$ source venv/bin/activate
   ```

That's all! You are in now. Cool, eh?

The command prompt is preceded by the virtual environment's name, so you can guess which environment is currently activated, which is shown in the screenshot that follows the code:

```
(venv)debian@beaglebone:~$
```

```
debian@beaglebone:~$ virtualenv --distribute --no-site-packages venv
The --no-site-packages flag is deprecated; it is now the default behavior.
New python executable in venv/bin/python
Installing distribute...............................................................
...................................................................................
.........................................done.
Installing pip...............done.
debian@beaglebone:~$ 
```

You can now install any package you want; it will only be accessible in the currently activated environment.

# Step 2 – installing MediaDrop

For installation, retrieve the last stable release from downloads:

```
(venv)debian@beaglebone:~$ mkdir MediaDrop
(venv)debian@beaglebone:~$ cd MediaDrop
(venv)debian@beaglebone:~/MediaDrop$ wget http://static.mediadrop.net/
releases/MediaCore-0.10.3.tar.gz
```

You can find all the releases at
http://static.mediadrop.net/releases/.

Then, perform the following steps:

1.  Extract the archive:

    ```
    (venv)debian@beaglebone:~/MediaDrop$ tar xvzf MediaCore-
    0.10.3.tar.gz
    ```

2.  Enter the new directory to launch the installation script:

    ```
    (venv)debian@beaglebone:~/MediaDrop$ cd MediaCore-0.10.3


    (venv)debian@beaglebone:~/MediaDrop/MediaCore-0.10.3$ python
    setup.py develop
    ```

3.  This will take a few minutes, as it checks and downloads the required dependencies, and will end with the following lines:

    ```
    Finished processing dependencies for MediaCore==0.10.3


    (venv)debian@beaglebone:~/MediaDrop/MediaCore-0.10.3$ cd ..


    (venv)debian@beaglebone:~/MediaDrop$
    ```

4.  From here, the recommended installation is to enter the following:

    ```
    (venv)debian@beaglebone:~/MediaDrop$ paster make-config MediaCore
    production.ini
    ```

This will generate the `production.ini` file, which the server will use as a configuration file. So, we can adapt by editing it.

# Step 3 – basic configuration file

What we want to do here is tell which database we created and the related credentials. So, edit the `production.ini` file, with `nano` (or `vim`) in order to focus on the [app:main] section, as we want to change the following line:

```
sqlalchemy.url = mysql://username:pass@localhost/dbname?charset=utf8&use_
unicode=0
```

The settings are shown in the following screenshot:

```
[DEFAULT]
email_to = you@yourdomain.com
smtp_server = localhost
error_email_from = paste@localhost

[server:main]
use = egg:Paste#http
host = 0.0.0.0
port = 8082

[app:main]
# Specify the database for SQLAlchemy to use
sqlalchemy.url = mysql://debian:temppwd@localhost/MediaDrop?charset=utf8&use_unicode=0
sqlalchemy.echo = False
sqlalchemy.pool_recycle = 3600
db.check_for_leaked_connections = False
```

At the same time, as port 8080 is already used, let's change this to an available port, something such as 8082. As you'll see later on, many servers use the 8080 port for their configuration settings, and obviously only one application will be able to use this port, which means that according to your configurations, you will have to decide which application will use the 8080 port.

> Additionally, you can eventually customize your configuration file with an e-mail that will let you receive notifications from the server. You will then need to install a local SMTP server and apply the settings in this `production.ini` file at the [DEFAULT] section.

Now, save and quit the editor. We are done with the configuration part.

# Step 4 – copying content from the initial data

We have completed all the configuration steps, and we are now going to deploy all the website data content.

To do this, copy the `data` directory from the sources to be at the same level as your `production.ini` file:

```
(venv)debian@beaglebone:~/MediaDrop$ cp -a MediaCore-0.10.3/data/.
```

Give it the write permissions for the `debian` user; when some content is uploaded, it will be written here:

```
(venv)debian@beaglebone:~/MediaDrop$ chmod 666 data
```

# Step 5 – filling the server database and contents

It's now time to fill the `MediaDrop` database we've created previously with some tables and required data. We just have to call a predefined command:

```
(venv)debian@beaglebone:~/MediaDrop$ paster setup-app deployment.ini
```

# Step 6 (optional) – full-text searching

Create some triggers that will allow you to have better searches than exact matches, as follows:

```
(venv)debian@beaglebone:~/MediaDrop$ mysql -u root -proot MediaDrop <
MediaCore-0.10.3/setup_triggers.sql
```

Nothing else is remaining; we are in. Time to start our first server!

# Testing time – "Hello Server"

You have a server that is waiting to be started locally:

```
(venv)debian@beaglebone:~/MediaDrop$ paster serve --reload production.ini
source env/bin/activate
```

```
(venv)debian@beaglebone:~/MediaDrop$ paster serve --reload deployment.ini
Starting subprocess with file monitor
Starting server in PID 6158.
serving on 0.0.0.0:8082 view at http://127.0.0.1:8082
```

You need to wait for the last line to be displayed before you move on, which means that the server is ready to answer the request.

> Take the example of your command, which ends with the following line of code:
>
> ```
> IOError: [Errno 2] No such file or directory: '/home/
> debian/production.ini'
> ```
>
> You might not be in the good path; using the `ls` command, check whether the `production.ini` file exists in the current directory.

Now, from anywhere on your local network, enter the address of your board with the defined port—for me, it's `192.168.0.15:8082`.

Welcome to your own new world; you should see the home page, as shown in the following screenshot:

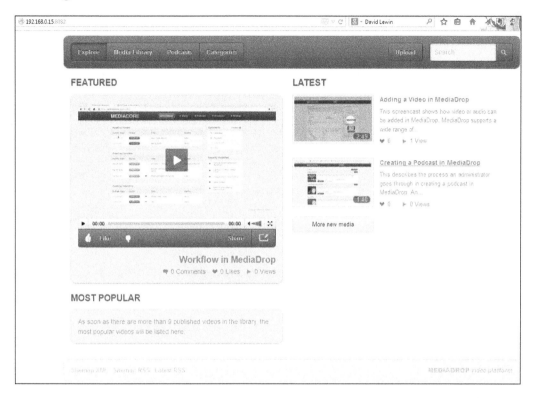

This is more than just a simple welcome screen; you also have some interesting videos that show you how to use your contents as well as how to add videos and podcasts, with examples.

You can even try and upload content right now if you want.

Currently, the server has been started manually. In *Chapter 4, Getting Your Own Video and Feeds*, we will see how to start the streaming service automatically on boot. This is a way to customize the boot process so that you know how to add a service such as MediaDrop at the start.

# Switching from development to production

Until now, we have been using the server as the `debian` user. This can be improved to better suit a server, which means that MediaDrop should be located at `/var/www` so that it is seen by the Apache server that is provided along with the Debian image for BeagleBone Black. We will just copy and adapt our previous experiments using the following commands:

```
(venv)debian@beaglebone:~/MediaDrop$ sudo mkdir /var/www/MediaDrop
(venv)debian@beaglebone:~/MediaDrop$ sudo cp -R MediaDrop/ /var/www
(venv)debian@beaglebone:~/MediaDrop$ cd /var/www/ MediaDrop/
```

As this is the final version, we don't need the sources in it:

```
(venv)debian@beaglebone:/var/www/MediaDrop$ sudo rm -fr MediaCore-0.10.3
```

We also grant the root user, as shown here:

```
(venv)debian@beaglebone:/var/www/MediaDrop$ sudo chmod 777 -R data
```

Finally, you can start the server as usual:

```
(venv)debian@beaglebone:/var/www/MediaDrop$ paster serve --reload
production.ini
```

```
(venv)debian@beaglebone:~/MediaDrop$ ls
MediaCore-0.10.3  MediaCore-0.10.3.tar.gz  data  production.ini
(venv)debian@beaglebone:~$ sudo mkdir /var/www/MediaDrop
(venv)debian@beaglebone:~$ sudo cp -R MediaDrop /var/www
(venv)debian@beaglebone:/var/www/MediaDrop SAVE$ ls
MediaCore-0.10.3_TEST  data  production.ini    mysql_script.sh  venv
(venv)debian@beaglebone:/var/www/MediaDrop$ rm -fr MediaCore-0.10.3
(venv)debian@beaglebone:/var/www/MediaDrop$ sudo chmod 777 -R data
(venv)debian@beaglebone:/var/www/MediaDrop$ paster serve --reload deployment.ini
Starting subprocess with file monitor
Starting server in PID 2903.
serving on 0.0.0.0:8082 view at http://127.0.0.1:8082
```

We are done with the configuration part, and you can now play around with the different settings if you wish, as this project has more to propose. For access to the complete documentation, go to `http://mediadrop.net/docs/`.

# Let's take a walk in our new MediaDrop server

The server is running well with you as the captain. No one else will try to look into your files and send you a warning about moderation or deletion. That being said, it also implies that no one else will manage the server for you. So what? Most of the default settings are fine; maybe a few of them need to be reset. We can take a quick look to explain what this is all about.

To access the admin interface, just add `admin` at the end of your address, as shown here:

```
http://192.168.0.15:8082/admin/
```

You will be asked for the default credentials:

```
User : admin
Password : admin
```

## Your first administrator action

As an administrator, the first thing you need to do is change the default password; this is the most obvious thing that an attacker will try, so go to **Users**, as shown in the following screenshot:

You should have a unique user: `admin`. Click on this to go to the user's profile in order to change the password.

 If you have defined an SMTP server, you will also be interested in filling in your e-mail in here.

Now, click on **Save**.

Now, let's go through some of the settings together; click on the **Settings** button to access the settings that are not related to rights, as shown here:

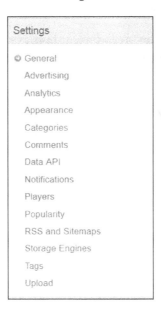

# General settings

In this section, you'll find everything related to the overall settings.

## Site name

Here, define the name of your website, which is not relevant if you are at home, but could be interesting if you deploy it for a company or to an external provider.

## Default language

If you'd like to change the language used in the pages, it's interesting to note that MediaDrop comes with a lot of choices, so you can surely find one that suits you.

## Appearance

This setting is used for the following actions:

- To customize the interface, such as colors and background images
- To display the login link for all the users
- To enable/disable buttons, such as **Share**, **Embed**, **Like**, and so on

The customization is really interesting here because you can use your own CSS, HTML header, and footer, so you can have a personalized interface.

# Categories

This part is important as you will need to enhance the provided categories for your needs.

While I won't explain what a category is, I can, however, say that there are useful combinations to create because a category can be related to another one as a child category, which lets you define subcategories. If all the users can use categories, only granted users will be able to define them. We will see how this is done in the next chapter.

In addition, an additional advantage is that categories are integrated during a textual search. This also includes entire sets of simple categories or more complex categories that can be made from a parent category, including many children categories.

# Comments

The following functions are related to comments:

- Allow or disable
- Functions related to your Facebook account (needs application ID)
- You might want all the comments to be approved before publication
- If you have an Akismet account, put your key in here so that the comments will be automatically filtered
- A dictionary, so you can add words to be filtered from the comments

# Notification e-mails

You can choose the type of events that you need to be warned about, as follows:

- **Media Uploaded**
- **Comment Posted**
- **Support Requested**

# Players

A list of players is provided with the server; these are capabilities that handle most of the media that a user will upload such as Vimeo, Youtube, DailyMotion, and so on.

I recommend that you allow all of them (click on the green light on the left-hand side) and define your preferred player using **Priority**, with arrows beside each player.

# Popularity

Each published video can be submitted to like/dislike votes. For your information and contrary to what one might think, *popularity* is not just the result of any addition/subtraction but it is a dedicated equation of the following form:

```
popularity_points = log_X(media.likes) + media.age/Y
```

This equation is clearly explained in the documentation at `http://mediadrop.net/docs/user/admin/settings.html#popularity`.

Both the decay exponent and lifetime are adaptable in this section.

# Tags

Tags are related to categories, but are nevertheless different. You can use them when you post a micro description of one or two words (recommended), but they are also useful for searches. Moreover, when users browse contents tags, they also help to get an overall opinion.

As with **Categories**, you need to have granted access in order to define tags.

# Upload

Here, you will find the setting that you might look after the most.

# File size limit

Indeed, there is a default 300 MB size limit for each upload, so you might end up with the following error, shown in the screenshot:

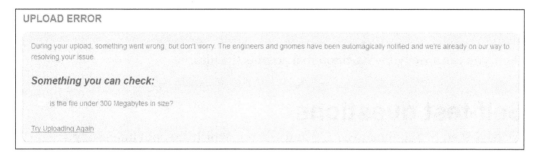

Don't confuse size limits and directory rights. What is the common thread between the two, you might ask? It's that if you forget to set the /data directory, you will have the same upload error when posting a link to a file.

# Storage engines

This is an important section under options that aims to list all the locations for the files, and mainly two of them need to be explained:

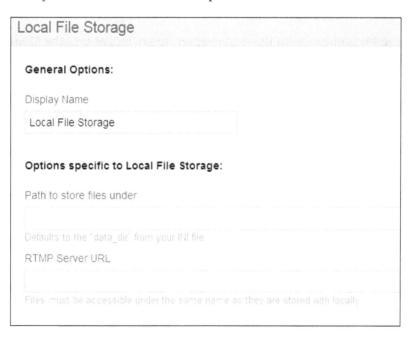

This points to the place where your content will be kept. This is really handy because you can modify the default partition scheme on BeagleBone if you have a local USB hard drive.

For a dedicated remote partition such as NFS or another type, there is:

*Remote URLs*

Here, you can specify the partition that accepts the files.

# Self-test questions

We have seen two commands, `find` and `locate`, which are both interesting. When you tried to use `find` and then `locate`, what difference did you notice in the results speed?

# Summary

We finally found what we were looking for: a simple way to publish any media in a local network. We can upload a video, picture, or music to be shared with just a few settings that are as easy as a mouse click. Thanks to this intuitive interface, you can skip the complicated settings while not sacrificing by paying an expensive fee. Once you have completed this part, you won't have to redo.

We are going to continue, with the next chapter, to go deeper into the MediaDrop server; we will explore the subjects that have been introduced here, such as submissions and daily tasks that will help you through automatic and social group notifications as well. This is where you will learn more about the administrator role.

# 2
# Media Management, Shares, and Social Activities

Now that the configuration is done, let's dive into the fun part. The MediaDrop web interface is intuitive enough to quickly access any required function. This chapter will introduce the main functionality and the concept of libraries as well as explain the workflow required to publish any of your media contents. Sharing media through social groups will also be introduced.

In this chapter, we will cover the following topics:

- How to use MediaDrop through workflows
- Why approvals are required
- How to get published
- Administrator tasks
- Exploring different ways to access your media

By the end of this chapter, you will be able to obtain a result similar to the one shown in the following screenshot:

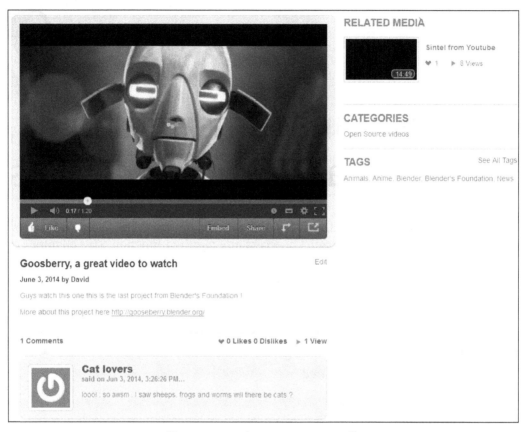

Yes, you can moderate comments as well

# How to use MediaDrop through workflows

You are here stamping your feet, waiting for your new embedded server to serve your goals and let the world know how cute your cat is. However, before doing this, you have to understand the workflow that MediaDrop uses.

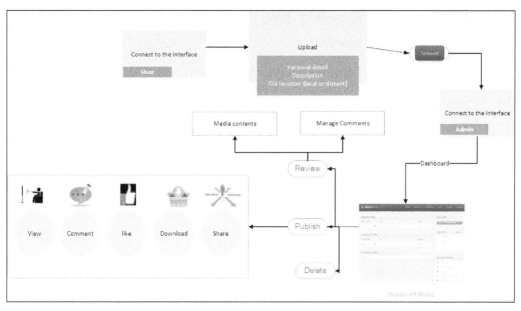

The way a user submits the media contents

When you need to publish content (files, URL, YouTube videos, and so on), you will need to go through some processes. Detailed here is an overall description we are going to see in detail:

- The user opens a connection to the server
- Then this user can create a personalized page with some text and pictures
- After submission, the administrator is notified that a new page has been created and is waiting for approbation
- The administrator then connects to a dashboard to apply different actions: **review**, **publish**, or **delete** this new page
- As soon as the page has been published, it is available on the server. This page can be viewed, commented, liked, shared, and so on.

# Why approvals are required

Using a media server is not similar to using a simple media reader, where you just copy/paste video or audio in it and read them later. Sharing contents implies that you can manage who will access them.

After submitting a video, it needs to be validated before it is made available online.

As such, consider these scenarios:

- You just came back from holidays and want to show your photos and videos to friends on your TV set and also let them add comments. *How about unrelated or inappropriate comments?*

- Your daughter would want to have her own space to publish her media and share it through Facebook from her laptop. *Don't you think this should be supervised a bit?*

- Meanwhile, your kid wants the last Disney movie from the VOD provider on his tablet, right now! *What about account credentials?*

 Standard media readers are DVDs, CDs, hard drives, **network attached storage** (**NAS**), game consoles, or any software/device that lets you listen to music or watch movies. The server we are going to set up replaces all of them with many additional capabilities.

These examples, taken from everyday life, are easy to implement with MediaDrop as long as you consider the BeagleBone Black server as the center of it all, instead of just being a media player.

# Publishing your media

When you first connect to the interface, simply click on **Upload**, as shown in the following screenshot. You will be redirected to the principal interface where you need to fill in the media details, as in the following screenshot.

- **The title of the post**: This will appear beside the thumbnail.

- **The author's name**: This will have implications related to user's rights.

- An email address.

- **A description**: To let your readers know what is it all about. Keep in mind that it will also be used when you share the post, so it's better to write explicitly.

- Optionally, you can also do the following:
    - Pick up some categories to define your upload group membership

° Add or use an existing tag for textual researches

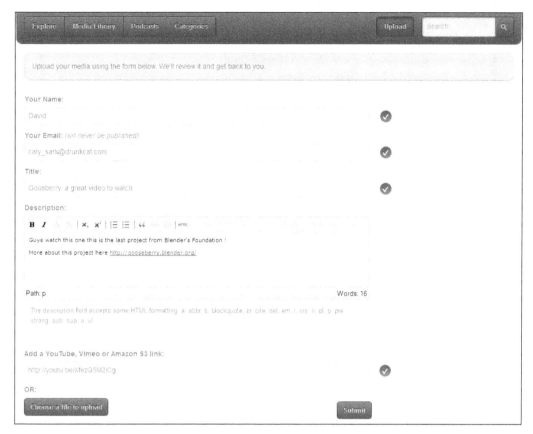

The post submitted for publication

Just pick the video from this location; in this case, this is a YouTube video, but it can come from your local PC, NAS, or even the BeagleBone Black itself through its USB access.

 Storing directly to the BeagleBone Black SD is not recommended because it doesn't have enough disk space for media files.

Now, click on the **Submit** button and a message will inform you that the post is submitted and is awaiting the administrator's approval.

If your media is a local file, the process will obviously be a little bit longer. A progress counter will appear, showing you the upload status (in percent) on the right-hand side of the screen. BeagleBone Black, being somewhat less reactive than a PC, ensures that you have reached 100 percent before going to the next step. Then, the type of file you intend to upload will be self detected.

# Auto administrated contents

Here, we have focused on how users will submit content. Nevertheless, if you are the sole user on your server, you might not want to bother with the whole workflow, so you can skip the user's steps. The modified workflow, as shown in the following figure, lets you publish your media content directly. Anyway, the same functionalities are accessible as for a standard user.

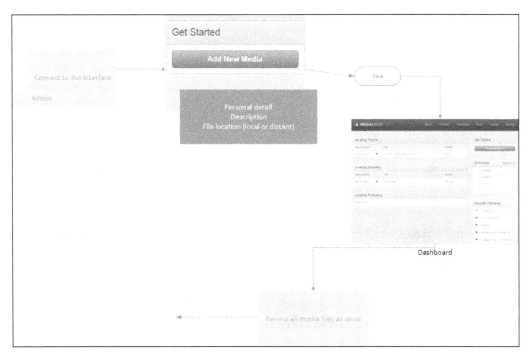

The workflow for self-published content

The user's submission part can be skipped by connecting as the administrator and directly clicking on the **Add New Media** button, as shown in the following screenshot:

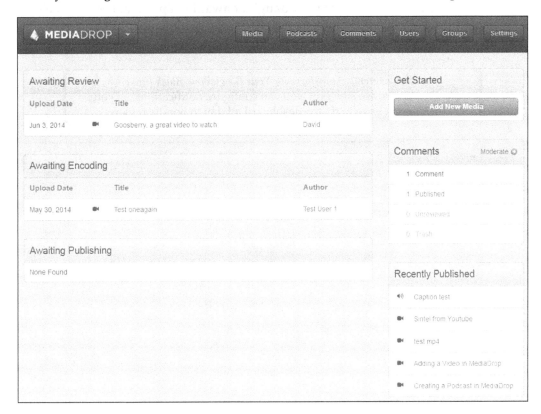

# Administrator tasks

This can be you in both the roles, or in many cases there is a dedicated person. In all the cases, administrator approval is required before the video is to be published.

The administrator who is connected to the dashboard page can see that some uploads are awaiting review.

 As you have seen in *Chapter 1, Transforming Your BeagleBone Black Into a Media Server*, this phase is related to the rights that each user has been granted.

You can also edit and publish as a user with administrator privileges.

The administrator is someone who is often busy with different tasks, and it's his responsibility to react in time to one's post. Professionals define this as *Quality of Service*. For example, this could be your daughter awaiting approval because she's sent a post from her iPad. No problem, even from the garden, you will be able to manage administration just from your tab.

 In *Chapter 1, Transforming Your BeagleBone Black Into a Media Server*, we saw how you can configure notifications, so you don't have to fix the dashboard all day to handle reviews.

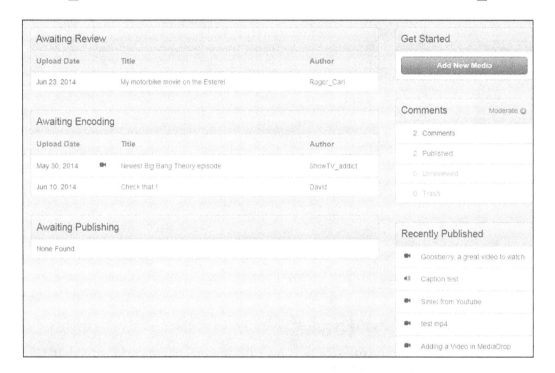

Each item that you click on from the **Awaiting Review** or **Awaiting Encoding** list will guide you to set this post's status to **Review Pending** (refer to the next screenshot). This is how you can manage the contents and set categories as tags for it.

MediaDrop often tries to extract pictures from the video as thumbnails; you might find appropriated choices if you pick one yourself from the **Upload image** button.

Your post might require some information, such as description, tags, and categories. Do keep in mind that when this post will be read, these details will help your readers to find and understand your content. So, while it is not mandatory, it's worthwhile having this completed. An example of one such description can be seen in the following screenshot:

You can click on **Save**—which is confirmed afterwards—and then validate with **Review Complete**. Finally, you can click on **Publish now** for the post to be published and can define it as **Published** for it to be available, as shown in the following screenshot:

There are more options to explore; for instance, you can define whether a file must be removed from publication (equivalent to *unpublished*) on a particular date, or you can even define the uploaded file's duration, resulting in an extract from the whole video.

Now, go to the MediaDrop listbox and select **View site**; and check whether as a user, you have obtained what you were expecting.

# Exploring different ways to access your media

When your content is in the **Published** status, MediaDrop generates dedicated links for you in the form of the following:

- A permalink to be used be in e-mails, websites, and so on. This kind of a link is generated, so will stay unchanged indefinitely.
- A Facebook post prepared with some of the details you already provided.
- A tweet with media information, including a link to your local content.

# Self-test questions

Q1. Video files can be big sometimes. Storing them on the SD card in most of the cases should be enough, but this might become a showstopper in some other cases. *Where should videos files indeed be stored?*

    1.   On the local flash.

    2.   On an external USB hard drive.

    3.   On a NAS or networked file system (NFS).

Q2. This chapter focused on video: *does this mean that only videos are supported?*

Q3. There are so many movie readers on the market, *"I don't need to bother with the contents' administration."* So what will I do:

    1.   I just need to share a video directory from my computer.

    2.   These are just video files, not banking accounts' credentials.

    3.   I prefer to protect my personal life and want my files to be watched by my neighbors or the rest of the world so, yes, it's worth spending a few minutes.

# Summary

In this chapter, we jumped from the administrator to the user's side of MediaDrop, so we covered contents management through simple process tasks that MediaDrop proposes.

Now, you know why you should select your user's rights carefully, so you don't need to worry about upload consequences. This means that you can be sure that any of your user's submitted content will have a delimited sharing perimeter: the one you have chosen.

As such, remember what Spiderman says:

> *"With great power comes great responsibility."*

We also saw that submissions can be done by many users or even by a single user, if necessary.

Fortunately, MediaDrop gets the security jobs done, as it is built around a user's privileges philosophy. That's why, in the next chapter, you will see how to manage your user's rights according to usages from some real-world examples.

# 3
# Examples of Real-world Situations

In the previous chapter, we looked at how we can use MediaDrop to publish our content. Now, we are going to discuss security, which is another important aspect of everyday life. You don't just ask the BeagleBone server to provide your content, but you also ask it to share this content the way you want. Here, you will see how security roles can ease administration tasks and how MediaDrop provides such a mechanism in the administrator console. To be as practical as possible, we will go through two scenarios and analyze them in a concrete manner: home and professional. The *home* scenario will be a good representation of the use cases that are encountered in everyday life, whereas the *professional* scenario will deal with use cases from a company where employees need to share media and access e-learning videos.

In this chapter, we will cover the following topics:

- Introducing the security role
- An everyday use case—a house in Springfield
- Second use case—media management in a company

# Introducing the security role

As we live in an interconnected world, we are exposed to misuses and attacks. As we will see in this chapter, security is of utmost importance irrespective of whether it's a small or large network. Even if role definitions require additional work, you should take the security of your network into consideration. Just like you fasten the seat belt in your car, you'd rather spend this extra time once and forget about it thereafter.

It can be summarized in 3 processes: write down all users who will require access, itemize what resources they will have access to, and then connect the dots between the lists. That's what we are going to see now.

# An everyday use case – a house in Springfield

*Home* will denote the scenario of a house in a town called Springfield where Bart lives with Homer as the administrator. Most of the use cases that might be encountered in everyday life have been gathered, as you can see in the picture.

The house is one of the greediest users of media you can find.

There are a desktop or laptop, computers, tablets, smartphones, gaming consoles, and connected TV, and our house project must use all of them at the same time. Nevertheless, you don't want to worry and spend your time on which user is connected to the tablet and what they are doing. While you have to manage these accesses, you'd certainly prefer to focus on the TV show and eventually take 5 minutes to allow the publication of some posts. You know how easy it is now.

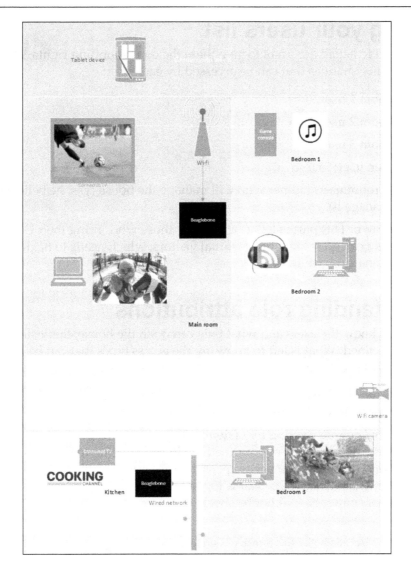

As shown in the preceding image, we can list some of the activities for the Springfield house's users. They want to:

- Watch movies
- Listen to music
- Have some podcasting
- Access online resources such as VOD/YouTube
- Install a Wi-Fi camera at the entrance

# Defining your users list

Now, we need to list all the users to give them the corresponding rights. This list defines the functionalities that can be accessed by each user:

- **Bedroom 1 user**: Bart
- **Bedroom 2 user**: Lisa
- **Bedroom 3 user**: Maggie
- **Kitchen user**: Marge
- **Main room user**: Homer who will manage the house (yes, he believes that he can manage it)
- **Unknown**: This part is left as a joker for those who "Bring their Own Device." This is a category for some eventual visitors, which needs to be defined in our scenario as well.

# Understanding role attributions

Now that you know the users and what they can do in the house, the security perimeter is defined. What is left to know are the access types that can be granted to these users. This list is a tool to understand the consequences for each role you assign:

- **Authenticated users**: These users just need to view and upload media. They only need (or want) to be granted minimum access.
- **Guests / people passing by / friends**: This is to allow your friends or some guests to access a part of your media without needing to log in. By setting this kind of access, you ensure privacy for yourself, as the embedded player will only be visible if the user is logged in. In this way, we make sure that if a visitor comes, he will not be shocked by Homer's contents.

 As each user has already been identified by a login to your local network, you already know that this user is granted access. This implies that anonymous users who might eventually try to connect can't access and obtain MediaDrop *guest* rights; therefore, they won't have access to any content, meaning they cannot post or read without your network's consent.

- **Power users**: These users can't do everything they want, as they inherit authenticated users' rights plus an additional ability to grant access to someone else. This role can be granted to anyone that you can rely on when you are unavailable for some administrator tasks. For the sake of the example, let's say this will be *Lisa*.

- **Administrator**: This is someone who is able to access the admin panel we have seen earlier in *Chapter 2, Media Management, Shares, and Social Activities*. If you want to keep your security strategy as stable as possible, there should be very few administrators: imagine everyone changing the access roles and granting access to *guests*, leading to a security breach.

# Group management

We now have all the prerequisites in place, so we can create our users in the house. What we are doing now is using the predefined groups of activities and setting users within these groups. Additionally, we are also creating our own group to see how easy it is.

To get started, connect to the admin console and select **Groups** on the interface so that you can see what rights are provided:

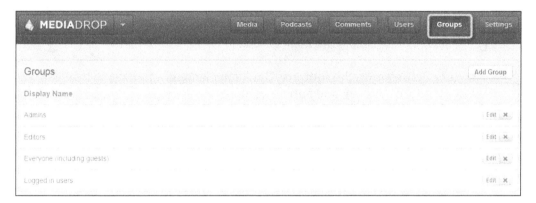

You can now associate the users with the predefined list of roles you want to grant them:

|  | Can view published media | Can upload new media | Grants the ability to upload new media | Grants access to edit site content | Grants access to the admin panel |
|---|---|---|---|---|---|
| Everyone (including guests) |  |  |  |  |  |
| Logged-in users |  |  |  |  |  |

|  | Can view published media | Can upload new media | Grants the ability to upload new media | Grants access to edit site content | Grants access to the admin panel |
|---|---|---|---|---|---|
| Editors |  |  |  |  |  |
| Admins |  |  |  |  |  |

Let's take a look at this table more closely:

- **Anonymous** people can view media, but we don't want them to upload new content, and most of all, they shouldn't be able to grant anything.

 Even though this is not about the protection of jewels, you don't want anyone to be able to set rights. This is obviously a security breach: anyone can grant other people the right to upload.

- **Logged-in users**, on the contrary, don't have enough privileges; they should at least be able to view and submit content
- **Editors** and **Admins** do their job correctly, so leave those as defined

We can see here that this doesn't fit our philosophy, so let's change the group settings to those used for our house. Let's bring in a few modifications:

|  | Can view published media | Can upload new media | Grants the ability to upload new media | Grants access to edit site content | Grants access to the admin panel |
|---|---|---|---|---|---|
| Everyone (including guests) |  |  |  |  |  |
| Logged-in users |  |  |  |  |  |
| Editors |  |  |  |  |  |
| Admins |  |  |  |  |  |

What we did is we assigned different roles to different people. **Editors** will be able to set upload and edit accesses, while **Admins** are allowed to play all the roles.

Most of the time, you won't need all these roles, so here we just stick to **Everyone**, **logged-in users**, or **Admin**. However, it is recommended that you set up all the roles for future use, as you might need to delegate **Editors** for extra emergent cases or even as a temporary role that can be removed later.

# Applying groups and users

The job is nearly done; only modifications are left to be set, which will only take a few minutes.

To define rights according to our house's strategy, we just have to modify the existing rights:

- **Everyone**: Click on the **Edit** button for this group, set only **View Published media** as checked, and click on **Save**
- Apply the related modifications for **Logged-in users** as well

What you need to do now is define your users; don't be surprised if just the **Admins** and **Editors** groups are proposed, as the **Logged-in** users and **Anonymous** are implicitly identifiable.

This should end as shown in the following screenshot:

We come to the end of the home scenario, resulting from our previous analysis and lists of users, actions, and roles.

 Most of the e-mails are real ones from the episodes; you can check this.

# Second use case – media management in a company

As we already saw how to organize roles in the previous topic, this part will focus more on the professional approach. With a very small budget compared to those that many IT departments require, we are nevertheless going to see how this solution can fit into professional contexts.

By taking a look at the following image and comparing it with the *home* scenario, we can see that the use cases for a company are organized into a different architecture in order to connect users. In addition, we can easily guess that the repartition of roles will be totally different because of the clear differences between departments.

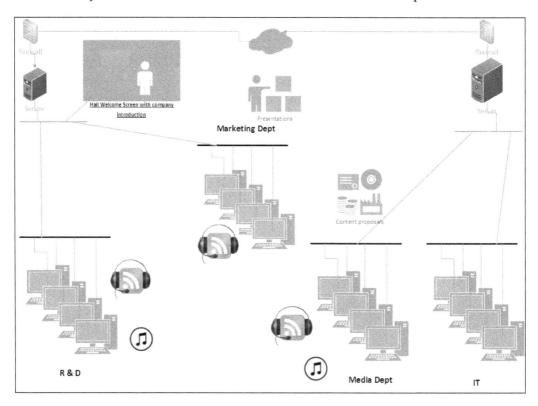

The company's network is now structured as "grapes" with dedicated subnetworks for each department's activities. As the IT manager, you have to define roles:

- **The welcome presentation**: This is a movie player for customers

- **Guests**: This gives your visitors and customers access to some of your content

- **R&D department**: This needs to listen to music, access company streaming contents (for example, e-learning), and podcasts

- **Media department**: This provides contents and podcasts

- **Marketing department**: This has access to movies (presentations) and podcasts

- **IT department**: In a word, you are responsible for administration, but this role can be split into many people

# Managing policies and groups

If you remember the table from the previous *home* scenario in the same *Group management* section, you might remember that we had quite the same repartition between users' types and their roles. Some differences remain, as we split more roles within our users; so, **Editors** will manage the site's contents only, while the **Uploader Admin** will manage upload attributions except the Editions ones.

|  | Can view published media | Can upload new media | Grants the ability to upload new media | Grants access to edit site content | Grants access to the admin panel |
|---|---|---|---|---|---|
| Everyone (including guests) |  |  |  |  |  |
| Logged-in users |  |  |  |  |  |
| Editors |  |  |  |  |  |
| Uploader Admin |  |  |  |  |  |
| Admins |  |  |  |  |  |

Therefore, with these exclusive roles, rights management is guaranteed, as only **Admins** will be able to get all the roles.

So, we will set some roles, as shown here:

| Users | | | | Add User |
|---|---|---|---|---|
| **Display Name** | **Email** | | **Group** | |
| Admin | chunkylover53@aol.com | | Admins | Edit ✖ |
| editor_master | imbusy@thecompany.com | | Editors | Edit ✖ |
| John Doe | marketing.user1@thecompany.com | | | Edit ✖ |
| Mediadept_user1 | Mediadept_user1@thecompany.com | | Upload admins | Edit ✖ |
| Stefany_market | Stefany@thecompany.com | | | Edit ✖ |
| upload_master | somewhere@overtherainbow.com | | Upload admins | Edit ✖ |
| User1_RnD | RnD1@thecompany.com | | Editors | Edit ✖ |

What we can see in the preceding screenshot is that a part of the administrative tasks can be shared with trusted people. So now take as an example the IT department being made up of the following roles:

- Admin
- Editor_master
- Upload_master

These roles also share some group attributions with the following:

- **User1_RnD**: **Editors**
- **Mediadept_user1**: **Upload Admins**

These have some delegating ability but not complete admin rights.

What about users such as John Doe from the marketing department and the presentation player in the hall? Actually, as they don't provide content, they don't need special user access; therefore, they just need to be *authenticated logged-in users*.

# Self-test questions

Q1. Where do you get users groups' settings?

1. In the Setting menu
2. In the groups menu
3. In the users Menu

Q2. True or false: In order to access a user's settings, you need to be logged in as an admin before accessing it.

Q3. If you want the user *Bart* to *watch and listen* to the house's contents, you will set his role as:

1.  Authenticated user
2.  Anonymous
3.  Administrator

Q4. True or false: Security requires enough additional time. Having an extra 10 minutes to obtain these details and write down lists is not useful. After all, your network already has some credentials

# Summary

We have been through a dense chapter. You might not be a security-passionate person, but it is most likely that you can now understand why you should consider this topic, and maybe your point of view might have changed. Hopefully you'll take a few minutes to define your security strategy based on the examples in this chapter.

Remember to find answers to the who, what, and how questions through the lists you have defined at the start so that you just need to set or use predefined roles in the **Groups** and user interfaces.

Using real-world and practical examples, we saw how the Springfield house is organized to let everyone be happy with media, in the bedroom or even in the garden.

We also saw how security can be applied to professional aspects as well, with the hope this part will help you the next time you need to apply a security strategy and architecture.

We will now leave the MediaDrop world to let you provide the content and become an actor yourself and share movies.

In the next chapter, we will be more creative, as we will set up our own content as well as services.

# 4

# Getting Your Own Video and Feeds

"One server to satisfy them all" could have been the name of this chapter. We now have a great media server where we can share any media, but we would like to be more independent so that we can choose the functionalities the server can have. The goal of this chapter is to let you cross the bridge, where you are going to increase your knowledge by getting your hands dirty. After all, you want to build your own services, so why not create your own contents as well.

More specifically, here we will begin by building a webcam streaming service from scratch, and we will see how this can interact with what we have implemented previously in the server. We will also see how to set up a service to retrieve RSS feeds. We will discuss the services in the following sections:

- Installing and running MJPG-Streamer
- Detecting the hardware device and installing drivers and libraries for a webcam
- Configuring RSS feeds with Leed

# Detecting the hardware device and installing drivers and libraries for a webcam

Even though today many webcams are provided with hardware encoding capabilities such as the Logitech HD Pro series, we will focus on those without this capability, as we want to have a low budget project. You will then learn how to reuse any webcam left somewhere in a box because it is not being used. At the end, you can then create a low cost video conference system as well.

## How to know your webcam

As you plug in the webcam, the Linux kernel will detect it, so you can read every detail it's able to retrieve about the connected device.

We are going to see two ways to retrieve the webcam we have plugged in: the easy one that is not complete and the harder one that is complete.

> *"All magic comes with a price."*
>
> –*Rumpelstiltskin, Once Upon a Time*

 Often, at a certain point in your installation, you have to choose between the easy or the hard way. Most of the time, powerful Linux commands or tools are not thought to be easy at first but after some experiments you'll discover that they really can make your life better.

Let's start with the fast and easy way, which is `lsusb` :

```
debian@arm:~$ lsusb
Bus 001 Device 002: ID 046d:0802 Logitech, Inc. Webcam C200
Bus 001 Device 001: ID 1d6b:0002 Linux Foundation 2.0 root hub
Bus 002 Device 001: ID 1d6b:0002 Linux Foundation 2.0 root hub
```

This just confirms that the webcam is running well and is seen correctly from the USB.

Most of the time we want more details, because a hardware installation is not exactly as described in books or documentations, so you might encounter slight differences. This is why the second solution comes in. Among some of the advantages, you are able to know each step that has taken place when the USB device was discovered by the board and Linux, such as in a hardware scenario:

```
debian@arm:~$ dmesg
```

```
usb 1-1: New USB device found, idVendor=046d, idProduct=0802
usb 1-1: New USB device strings: Mfr=0, Product=0, SerialNumber=2
usb 1-1: SerialNumber: 42E6B390
usb 1-1: usb_probe_device
usb 1-1: configuration #1 chosen from 1 choice
usb 1-1: adding 1-1:1.0 (config #1, interface 0)
usb 1-1: adding 1-1:1.1 (config #1, interface 1)
usb 1-1: adding 1-1:1.2 (config #1, interface 2)
usb 1-1: adding 1-1:1.3 (config #1, interface 3)
hub 1-0:1.0: state 7 ports 1 chg 0000 evt 0002
hub 1-0:1.0: port 1 enable change, status 00000503
uvcvideo 1-1:1.0: usb_probe_interface
uvcvideo 1-1:1.0: usb_probe_interface - got id
uvcvideo: Found UVC 1.00 device <unnamed> (046d:0802)
input: UVC Camera (046d:0802) as /devices/ocp.3/47400000.usb/musb-hdrc.1.auto/usb1/1-1/1-1:1.0/input/input1
usbcore: registered new interface driver uvcvideo
USB Video Class driver (1.1.1)
snd-usb-audio 1-1:1.2: usb_probe_interface
snd-usb-audio 1-1:1.2: usb_probe_interface - got id
```

A UVC device (here, a Logitech C200) has been used to obtain these messages

Most probably, you won't exactly have the same outputs, but they should be close enough so that you can interpret them easily when they are referred to:

- **New USB device found**: This is the main message. In case of any issue, we will check its presence elsewhere. This message indicates that this is a hardware error and not a software or configuration error that you need to investigate.

- **idVendor** and **idProduct**: This message indicates that the device has been detected. This information is interesting so you can check the constructor detail.

 Most recent webcams are compatible with the Linux USB Video Class (UVC), you can check yours at http://www.ideasonboard.org/uvc/#devices.

- Among all the messages, you should also look for the one that says **Registered new interface driver interface** because failing to find it can be a clue that Linux could detect the device but wasn't able to install it.

 The new device will be detected as /dev/video0. Nevertheless, at start, you can see your webcam as a different device name according to your BeagleBone configuration, for example, if a video capable cape is already plugged in.

# Setting up your webcam

Now we know what is seen from the USB level. The next step is to use the crucial *Video4Linux* driver, which is like a Swiss army knife for anything related to video capture:

```
debian@arm:~$ Install v4l-utils
```

The primary use of this tool is to inquire about what the webcam can provide with some of its capabilities:

```
debian@arm:~$ v4l2-ctl --all
```

There are four distinctive sections that let you know how your webcam will be used according to the current settings:

- Driver info (1) : This contains the following information:
    - Name, vendor, and product IDs that we find in the system message
    - The driver info (the kernel's version)
    - Capabilities: the device is able to provide video streaming

- Video capture supported format(s) (2): This contains the following information:

    ○ What resolution(s) are to be used. As this example uses an old webcam, there is not much to choose from but you can easily have a lot of choices with devices nowadays.

    ○ The pixel format is all about how the data is encoded but more details can be retrieved about format capabilities (see the next paragraph).

    ○ The remaining stuff is relevant only if you want to know in precise detail.

- Crop capabilities (3): This contains your current settings. Indeed, you can define the video crop window that will be used. If needed, use the crop settings:

    ```
    --set-crop-output=top=<x>,left=<y>,width=<w>,height=<h>
    ```

- Video input (4): This contains the following information:

    ○ The input number. Here we have used 0, which is the one that we found previously.

    ○ Its current status.

    ○ The famous *frames per second*, which gives you a local ratio. This is not what you will obtain when you'll be using a server, as network latencies will downgrade this ratio value.

You can grab capabilities for each parameter. For instance, if you want to see all the video formats the webcam can provide, type this command:

```
debian@arm:~$ v4l2-ctl --list-formats
```

```
debian@arm:~/mjpg-streamer/mjpg-streamer-code/mjpg-streamer-experimental$ v4l2-ctl --list-formats
ioctl: VIDIOC_ENUM_FMT
        Index        : 0
        Type         : Video Capture
        Pixel Format: 'YUYV'
        Name         : YUV 4:2:2 (YUYV)

        Index        : 1
        Type         : Video Capture
        Pixel Format: 'MJPG' (compressed)
        Name         : MJPEG
```

Here, we see that we can also use MJPEG format directly provided by the cam.

While this part is not mandatory, such a hardware tour is interesting because you know what you can do with your device. It is also a good habit to be able to retrieve diagnostics when the webcam shows some bad signs.

If you would like to get more in depth knowledge about your device, install the **uvcdynctrl** package, which lets you retrieve all the formats and frame rates supported.

# Installing and running MJPG-Streamer

Now that we have checked the chain from the hardware level up to the driver, we can install the software that will make use of *Video4Linux* for video streaming. Here comes *MJPG-Streamer*.

This application aims to provide you with a JPEG stream on the network available for browsers and all video applications.

Besides this, we are also interested in this solution as it's made for systems with less advanced CPU, so we can start MJPG-Streamer as a service. With this streamer, you can also use the built-hardware compression and even control webcams such as pan, tilt, rotations, zoom capabilities, and so on.

## Installing MJPG-Streamer

Before installing MJPG-Streamer, we will install all the necessary dependencies:

```
debian@arm:~$ install subversion libjpeg8-dev imagemagick
```

Next, we will retrieve the code from the project:

```
debian@arm:~$ svn checkout http://svn.code.sf.net/p/mjpg-streamer/code/
mjpg-streamer-code
```

You can now build the executable from the sources you just downloaded by performing the following steps:

1. Enter the following into the local directory you have downloaded:

   ```
   debian@arm:~$ cd mjpg-streamer-code/mjpg-streamer
   ```

2. Then enter the following command:

   ```
   debian@beaglebone:~/mjpg-streamer-code/mjpg-streamer$ make
   ```

When the compilation is complete, we end up with some new files. From this picture the new green files are produced from the compilation: there are the executables and some plugins as well.

That's all that is needed, so the application is now considered ready. We can now try it out. Not so much to do after all, don't you think?

# Starting the application

This section aims at getting you started quickly with MJPG-Streamer. At the end, we'll see how to start it as a service on boot.

Before getting started, the server requires some plugins to be copied into the dedicated `lib` directory for this purpose:

**debian@beaglebone:~/mjpg-streamer-code/mjpg-streamer$ sudo cp input_uvc. so output_http.so /usr/lib**

The MJPG-Streamer application has to know the path where these files can be found, so we define the following environment variable:

**debian@beaglebone:~/mjpg-streamer-code/mjpg-streamer$ export LD_LIBRARY_ PATH=/usr/lib;$LD_LIBRARY_PATH**

Enough preparation! Time to start streaming:

**debian@beaglebone:~/mjpg-streamer-code/mjpg-streamer$./mjpg_streamer -i "input_uvc.so" -o "output_http.so -w www"**

```
debian@arm:~/mjpg-streamer/mjpg-streamer-code/mjpg-streamer$ ./mjpg_streamer $./mjpg_streamer -i "input_uvc.so" -o "output_http.so -w www"
MJPG Streamer Version: svn rev: 3:182
DBG(input_uvc.c, input_init(), 136): argv[0]=UVC webcam grabber
DBG(input_uvc.c, input_init(), 302): input id: 0
i: Using V4L2 device.: /dev/video0
i: Desired Resolution: 640 x 480
i: Frames Per Second.: not limited
i: Format............: JPEG
i: TV-Norm...........: DEFAULT
o: www-folder-path...: ./www/
o: HTTP TCP port.....: 8080
o: username:password.: disabled
o: commands..........: enabled
```

As the script starts, the input parameters that will be taken into consideration are displayed. You can now identify this information, as they have been explained previously:

- The detected device from V4L2
- The resolution that will be displayed, according to your settings
- Which port will be opened
- Some controls that depend on your camera capabilities (tilt, pan, and so on)

If you need to change the port used by *MJPG-Streamer*, add -p xxxx at the end of the command, which is shown as follows:

```
debian@beaglebone:~/mjpg-streamer-code/mjpg-streamer$
./mjpg_streamer -i "input_uvc.so" -o "output_http.so -w
www -p 1234"
```

## Let's add some security

If you want to add some security, then you should set the credentials:

```
debian@beaglebone:~/mjpg-streamer-code/mjpg-streamer$ ./mjpg-streamer -o
"output_http.so -w ./www -c debian:temppwd"
```

Credentials can always be stolen and used without your consent. The best way to ensure that your stream is confidential all along would be to encrypt it.

So if you intend to use strong encryption for secured applications, the crypto-cape is worth taking a look at

```
http://datko.net/2013/10/03/howto_crypto_
beaglebone_black/.
```

## "I'm famous" – your first stream

That's it. The webcam is made accessible to everyone across the network from BeagleBone; you can access the video from your browser and connect to http://192.168.0.15:8080/.

You will then see the default welcome screen, bravo!:

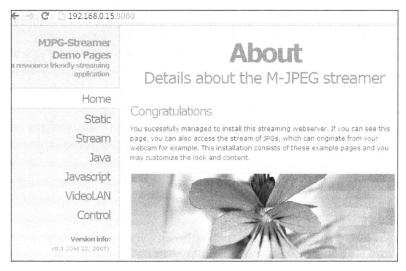

Your first contact with the MJPG-Server

 You might wonder how you would get informed about which port to use among those already assigned. Then teleport yourself to *Appendix A*.

# Using our stream across the network

Now that the webcam is available across the network, you have several options to handle this:

- You can use the direct flow available from the home page. On the left-hand side menu, just click on the **stream** tab.

- Using VLC, you can open the stream with the direct link available at `http://192.168.0.15:8080/?action=stream`.

  The **VideoLAN** menu tab is a M3U-playlist link generator that you can click on. This will generate a playlist file you can open thereafter.

 In this case, VLC is efficient, as you can transcode the webcam stream to any format you need. Although it's not mandatory, this solution is the most efficient, as it frees the BeagleBone's CPU so that your server can focus on providing services.

- Using MediaDrop, we can integrate this new stream in our shiny MediaDrop server, knowing that currently MediaDrop doesn't support direct local streams. You can create a new post with the related URL link in the message body, as shown in the following screenshot:

# Starting the streaming service automatically on boot

In the beginning, we saw that MJPG-Streamer needs only one command line to be started. We can put it in a bash script, but servicing on boot is far better. For this, use a console text editor – nano or vim – and create a file dedicated to this service. Let's call it start_mjpgstreamer and add the following commands:

```
#! /bin/sh
# /etc/init.d/start_mjpgstreamer

export LD_LIBRARY_PATH="/home/debian/mjpg-streamer/mjpg-streamer-code/
mjpg-streamer;$LD_LIBRARY_PATH"
EXEC_PATH="/home/debian/mjpg-streamer/mjpg-streamer-code/mjpg-streamer"

$EXEC_PATH/mjpg_streamer -i "input_uvc.so" -o "output_http.so -w EXEC_
PATH /www"
```

You can then use administrator rights to add it to the services:

```
debian@arm:~$ sudo /etc/init.d/start_mjpgstreamer start
```

On the next reboot, MJPG-Streamer will be started automatically.

# Exploring new capabilities to install

For those about to explore, we salute you!

As the book is not just about installation and configuration, I thought that it would be useful to play around with what we just installed in the previous chapters, such as getting into the plugins in more depth or, why not, a different service with the webcam.

# Plugins

Remember that at the beginning of this chapter, we began the demonstration with two plugins:

```
debian@beaglebone:~/mjpg-streamer-code/mjpg-streamer$ ./mjpg_streamer -i
"input_uvc.so" -o "output_http.so -w www"
```

If we take a moment to look at these plugins, we will understand that the first plugin is responsible for handling the webcam directly from the driver.

Simply ask for help and options as follows:

```
debian@beaglebone:~/mjpg-streamer-code/mjpg-streamer$ ./mjpg_streamer
--input "input_uvc.so --help"
```

```
MJPG Streamer Version: svn rev: 3:182
 DBG(input_uvc.c, input_init(), 136): argv[0]=UVC webcam grabber
 DBG(input_uvc.c, input_init(), 136): argv[1]=--help
 DBG(input_uvc.c, input_init(), 186): case 0,1
 ---------------------------------------------------------------
 Help for input plugin..: UVC webcam grabber
 ---------------------------------------------------------------
 The following parameters can be passed to this plugin:

 [-d | --device ].......: video device to open (your camera)
 [-r | --resolution ]...: the resolution of the video device,
                          can be one of the following strings:
                          QSIF QCIF CGA QVGA CIF VGA
                          SVGA XGA SXGA
                          or a custom value like the following
                          example: 640x480
 [-f | --fps ]..........: frames per second
                          (activates YUYV format, disables MJPEG)
 [-m | --minimum_size ].: drop frames smaller then this limit, useful
                          if the webcam produces small-sized garbage frames
                          may happen under low light conditions
 [-n | --no_dynctrl ]...: do not initalize dynctrls of Linux-UVC driver
 [-l | --led ]..........: switch the LED "on", "off", let it "blink" or leave
                          it up to the driver using the value "auto"
 ---------------------------------------------------------------

 [-t | --tvnorm ] ......: set TV-Norm pal, ntsc or secam
 ---------------------------------------------------------------
```

The second plugin is about the web server settings:

- The path to the directory contains the final web server HTML pages. This implies that you can modify the existing pages with a little effort or create new ones based on those provided.

- Force a special port to be used. Like I said previously, port use is dedicated for a server. You define here which will be the one for this service.

- You can discover many others by asking:

```
debian@arm:~$ ./mjpg_streamer --output "output_http.so  --help"
```

```
debian@arm:~/mjpg-streamer/mjpg-streamer-code/mjpg-streamer$ ./mjpg_streamer --output "output_http.so --help"
MJPG Streamer Version: svn rev: 3:182
---------------------------------------------------------------
Help for output plugin..: HTTP output plugin
---------------------------------------------------------------
The following parameters can be passed to this plugin:

[-w | --www ]...........: folder that contains webpages in
                          flat hierarchy (no subfolders)
[-p | --port ]..........: TCP port for this HTTP server
[-c | --credentials ]...: ask for "username:password" on connect
[-n | --nocommands ]....: disable execution of commands
---------------------------------------------------------------
```

 Apart from **input_uvc** and **output_http,** you have other available plugins to play with. Let's take a look at the *plugins* directory.

# Another tool for the webcam

The `Mjpg_streamer` project is dedicated for streaming over network, but it is not the only one. For instance, do you have any specific needs such as monitoring your house/son/cat/Jon Snow figurine?

 *buuuuzzz*: if you answered *yes* to the last one, you just defined yourself as a geek.

Well, in that case the `Motion` project is for you; just install the *motion* package and start it with the default `motion.conf` configuration. You will then record videos and pictures of any moving object/person that will be detected. As *MJPG-Streamer* motion aims to be a low CPU consumer, it works very well on BeagleBone Black.

# Configuring RSS feeds with Leed

Our server can handle videos, pictures, and music from any source and it would be cool to have another tool to retrieve news from some RSS providers. This can be done with Leed, a RSS project organized for servers. You can have a final result, as shown in the following screenshot:

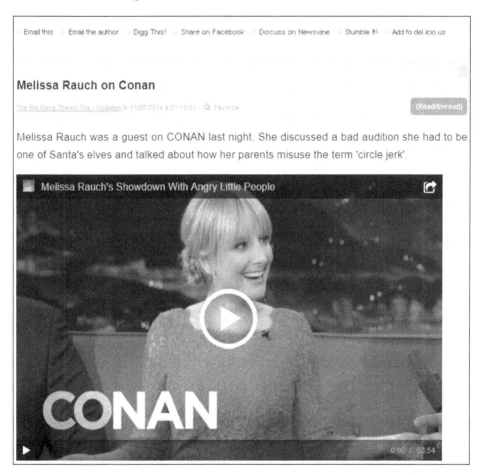

This project has a "quick and easy" installation spirit, so you can give it a try without harness. Leed (for Light Feed) allows you to you access RSS feeds from any browser, so no RSS reader application is needed, and every user in your network can read them as well. You install it on the server and feeds are automatically updated.

 Well, the truth behind the scenes is that a `cron` task does this for you. You will be guided to set some synchronisation after the installation.

# Creating the environment for Leed in three steps

We already have Apache, MySQL, and PHP installed, and we need a few other prerequisites to run Leed:

1. Create a database for Leed
2. Download the project code and set permissions
3. Install Leed itself

## Creating a database for Leed

Remember the database that we created for MediaDrop in *Chapter 1, Transforming Your BeagleBone Black into a Media Server*?

You will be at ease here, as this is exactly the same approach because Leed requires its own database as well.

You will begin by opening a MySQL session:

```
debian@arm:~$ mysql -u root -p
```

**What we need here is to have a dedicated Leed user with its database. This user will be connected using the following:**

```
create user 'debian_leed'@'localhost' IDENTIFIED BY 'temppwd';
create database leed_db;
use leed_db;
grant create, insert, update, select, delete on leed_db.* to debian_leed@
localhost;
exit
```

```
mysql> create user 'debian_leed'@'localhost' IDENTIFIED BY 'temppwd';
Query OK, 0 rows affected (0.00 sec)

mysql> create database leed_db;
Query OK, 1 row affected (0.21 sec)

mysql> use leed_db;
Database changed
mysql> grant create, insert, update, select, delete on leed_db.* to debian_leed@localhost;
Query OK, 0 rows affected (0.00 sec)

mysql> exit
Bye
debian@beaglebone:~$
```

# Downloading the project code and setting permissions

We prepared our server to have its environment ready for Leed, so after getting the latest version, we'll get it working with Apache by performing the following steps:

1. From your *home*, retrieve the latest project's code. It will also create a dedicated directory:

   ```
   debian@arm:~$ git clone https://github.com/1dleman/Leed.git
   debian@arm:~$ ls
   mediadrop mjpg-streamer Leed music
   ```

2. Now, we need to put this new directory where the Apache server can find it:

   ```
   debian@arm:~$ sudo mv Leed /var/www/
   ```

3. Change the permissions for the application:

   ```
   debian@arm:~$ chmod 777 /var/www/Leed/ -R
   ```

# Installing Leed

When you go to the server address (`http//192.168.0.15/leed/install.php`), you'll get the following installation screen:

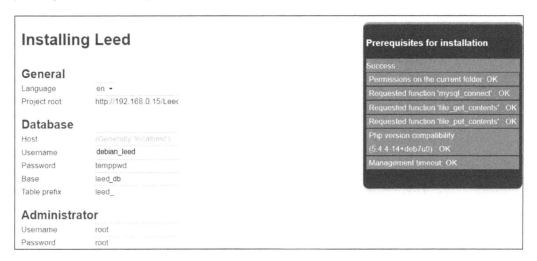

We now need to fill in the database details that we previously defined and add the *Administrator* credentials as well. Now save and quit. Don't worry about the explanations, we'll discuss these settings thereafter.

It's important that all items from the *prerequisites* list on the right are green.

Otherwise, a warning message will be displayed about the wrong permissions settings, as shown in the following screenshot:

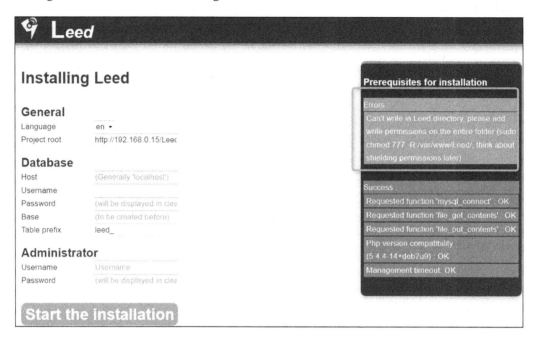

After the configuration, the installation is complete:

Leed is now ready for you.

# Setting up a cron job for feed updates

If you want automatic updates for your feeds, you'll need to define a synchronization task with `cron`:

1. Modify `cron` jobs:

   ```
   debian@arm:~$ sudo crontab -e
   ```

2. Add the following line:

```
0 * * * * wget -q -O /var/www/leed/logsCron "http://192.168.0.15/
Leed/action.php?action=synchronize
```

3. Save it and your feeds will be refreshed every hour.

4. Finally, some little cleanup: remove `install.php` for security matters:

```
debian@arm:~$ rm /var/www/Leed/install.php
```

# Using Leed to add your RSS feed

When you need to add some feeds from the **Manage** menu, in **Feed Options** (on the right- hand side) select **Preferences** and you just have to paste the RSS link and add it with the button:

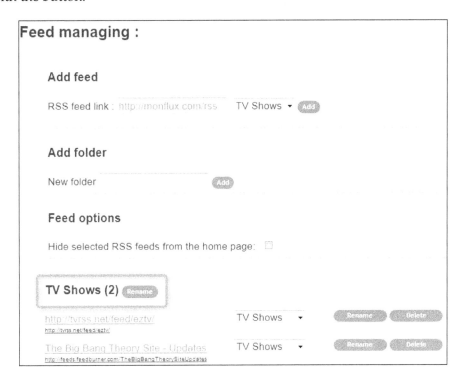

You might find it useful to organize your feeds into groups, as we did for movies in MediaDrop. The **Rename** button will serve to achieve this goal. For example, here a **TV Shows** category has been created, so every feed related to this type will be organized on the main screen.

# Some Leed preferences settings in a server environment

You will be asked to choose between two synchronisation modes: **Complete** and **Graduated**.

- **Complete**: This is to be used in a usual computer, as it will update *all* your feeds in a row, which is a CPU consuming task

- **Graduated**: Look for the oldest 10 feeds and update them if required

You also have the possibility of allowing anonymous people to read your feeds. If you remember, in *Chapter 3, Examples of Real-world Situations*, we allowed guests to access our content but not to publish any. This is the same case here. Setting **Allow anonymous readers** to **Yes** will let your guests access your feeds but not add any.

# Extending Leed with plugins

If you want to extend Leed capabilities, you can use the *Leed Market* — as the author defined it — from **Feed options** in the **Manage** menu. There, you'll be directed to the Leed Market space. Installation is just a matter of downloading the ZIP file with all plugins:

```
debian@arm:~/Leed$  wget  https://github.com/ldleman/Leed-market/archive/
master.zip
debian@arm:~/Leed$ sudo unzip master.zip
```

Let's use the AdBlock plugin for this example:

1.  Copy the content of the AdBlock plugin directory where Leed can see it:

    ```
    debian@arm:~/Leed$ sudo cp -r Leed-market-master/adblock /var/www/
    Leed/plugins
    ```

2. Connect yourself and set the plugin by navigating to **Manage | Available Plugins** and then activate adblock with **Enable**, as follows:

## Plugins :

You can download and install new plugins for free : Leed Market.

### Installed plugins :

**Name:** Adblock
**Author:** Phyks
**LICENCE:** BEERWARE (See README.md file)
**Version:** 2.2.1
**Website:** http://www.phyks.me

The adblock plugin for leed allows to block embedded flash contents and / or images in feeds. You can set it fine-grained for each feed. You can also disable images only for mobile devices.

( Enable )

**Name:** Delete the Cache
**Author:** qwerty
**LICENCE:** Tea Licence
**Version:** 1.0.1
**Website:** http://etudiant-libre.fr.nf

Vide le cache

( Enable )

In this chapter, we covered:

- Some words about the hardware
- How to know your webcam
- Configuring RSS feeds with Leed

# Summary

In this chapter, we had some good experiments with the hardware part of the server "from the ground," to finally end by successfully setting up the webcam service on boot. We discovered hardware detection, a way to "talk" with our local webcam and thus to be able to see what happens when we plug a device in the BeagleBone.

Through the topics, we also discovered *video4linux* to retrieve information about the device, and learned about configuring devices. Along the way, we encountered *MJPG-Streamer*. Finally, it's better to be on our own instead of being dependent on some GUI interfaces, where you always wonder where you need to click. Finally, our efforts have been rewarded, as we ended up with a web page we can use and modify according to our tastes.

RSS news can also be provided by our server so that you can manage all your feeds in one place, read them anywhere, and even organize dedicated groups.

Plenty of concepts have been seen for hardware and software. Then think of this chapter as a concrete example you can use and adapt to understand how Linux works.

I hope you enjoyed this freedom of choice, as you drag ideas and drop them in your BeagleBone as services. We entered in the DIY area, showing you ways to explore further. You can argue, saying that we can choose the software but still use off the shelf commercial devices.

Looking for more independence? Good! In the next chapter, we will see how to build a more personalized object, something that will resemble your choices: your own player device.

# 5
# Building Your Media Player

As shown in the previous chapters, the BeagleBone Black board can do much more than provide media and services. It can be adapted to a wide range of projects you have in mind. Moreover, we'll see how this board differs from others with respect to design. You'll be introduced to the concept of add-ons, so you will know how to choose a functional brick that can be used in one of your projects. At the end of this chapter, you'll see how to get your project up and running. This is the chapter where we can have some fun, so let's get our brain on fire!

In this chapter, we will cover the following topics:

- Introducing BeagleBone capes
- Your own media player in your hands
- Installing a system for the expansion board
- Using the expansion board with Android

## Introducing BeagleBone capes

In the first chapter, we said that the richness of a system relies mainly on its ecosystem. For example, the OS of a computer, such as Windows, Mac OS, or Linux, can be used not only for the graphical interface but also for the wide range of applications that you can install. This is quite similar to the embedded world, where a large choice of boards might confuse you quickly; you need to choose a CPU, OS, supported applications, programming languages that can be used on it, documentations, and so on. The list can be quite long depending on your final project.

A good criterion to look out for in a board is its expansion capability: the feature where one can add some more functionality to a board, such as plugins to software. In this sense, our board has a lot of features to propose. In the BeagleBone world, these add-ons are called **capes**.

Here's a definition of capes according to the creators of BeagleBone:

> *Adding cape plug-in boards to the popular BeagleBone computer allows hobbyists, makers and developers to quickly and easily augment BeagleBone's capabilities with LCD screens, motor control and battery power as well as the ability to create their own circuits*

This hardware openness lets you add functional boards, as you'd do from the application markets (the Apple store, Google Play, and so on) and thus enables you to add any functionality for your projects. You just have to plug your cape onto the two expansion connectors so that it is directly powered and recognized by the system. For a good overview, take a look at the capes' wiki page, available at `http://elinux.org/Beagleboard:BeagleBone_Capes`.

Here, you will find documentations and presentations from professionals and hobbyists who have designed capes.

# Exploring capes' categories

At the beginning of BeagleBone Black, the Wiki was composed of 20 capes that weren't compatible with the Black series. At the time of writing this book, this list has grown to 77 capes with 51 capes for BeagleBone Black; this gives us an idea of the community's effort behind this market. Here's an extract:

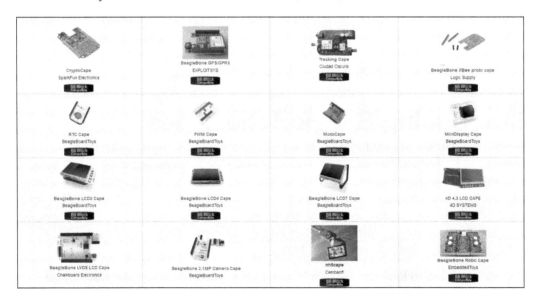

It's not possible to group all the capes in distinct categories, as some of them are conceptual. Anyway, to give you an idea, these capes mostly propose the following features:

- Wi-Fi
- Audio
- Power (PowerBar and the Power Supply cape are useful for autonomous projects)
- Displays (*mini displays*, *LCD3*, *LCD4*, and *LCD7*)
- An extension board with a display (*4D capes*)

For the *others/miscellaneous* category:

- **Crypto cape**: A very interesting cape that you can use to add serious security measures to your server or your applications. According to the author:

    *This cape will offload the CPU for cryptographic operations (usefully for a networked device that makes heavy use of VPN/TLS/SSL). It can also be used to enhance the security of an existing project with hardware RSA, ECC, SHA-2, a RTC, additional EEPROM*

- Prototyping (breadboards, *protoboard*).
- "All in one," which includes different functionalities, sensors or actuator drivers such as the **GVS** cape (GVS stands for **Ground, Voltage, and Signal**).
- Robotic and I/O (*Robocape*, *industrial I/O cape*).
- ADC, PWM, Analog, dual relays, smart relays.
- Interfacing capes (for Arduino shield, mikroBUS).

No matter what you choose, before considering a cape you must look for the **BB Black Compatible** logo, as shown here:

This guarantees that the cape you buy will work with your board.

# Considering a personal Palm Media player

This part of the chapter deals with how you can build a media player for yourself using the concept of capes, which you've just been introduced to. From the long list of available capes, we'll use the BeagleBone Black Expansion board from Chipsee.

From the two versions of this expansion board—resistive and capacitive—we will use the capacitive version, which has a five-point multitouch.

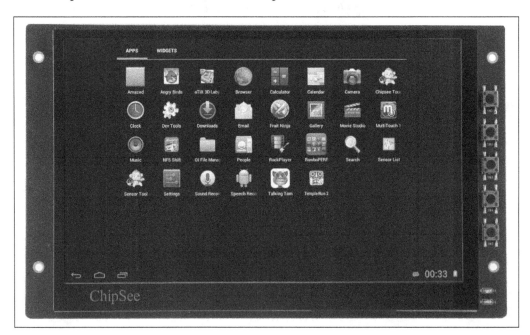

# Functional description

If you take a look at the functionalities that this expansion board proposes, it will give you an idea of why this is more than a display:

- A 7-inch screen with a resolution of 1024 x 600 pixels
- Capable of 5-point detection
- One audio out and one mic in
- Two RS232 ports
- One RS485 port
- Two analog channels
- 1 CAN port
- 1 integrated buzzer
- Five user keys
- Two user LEDs (green and blue)
- One embedded 3-axis accelerometer

# Physical description

On the reverse side of the board, you can see the following components (also shown in the following screenshot):

1. A multifunction connector with communication, acquisition, and power connections. You'll find the same signals from COM1 (Tx, Rx) and an additional COM port UART2 that is shared with RS485 #1, an additional port RS482 #2, and finally a **Control Area Network (CAN)**, which is a network designed to be used in industrial conditions.

2. The COM1 serial port, which has been changed from its original implementation. The provided systems are configured to debug to UART1 instead of UART0 on the BeagleBone, including a hardware driver. This implies that you can directly connect a serial terminal to the DB9 connector.

3. Power and reset buttons (coming from BeagleBone for accessibility).

4. Buzzer.

5. JTAG connector.

6. P8 header.

7. P9 header.

8. Audio output/microphone input (blue- and rose-colored, respectively).

9. The boot switch, which allows you to choose between the SD card (up) or eMMC boot (down).

10. Power: 5V/2A DC input is used for BeagleBone as for all the expansion board's needs. You don't need any additional adapters.

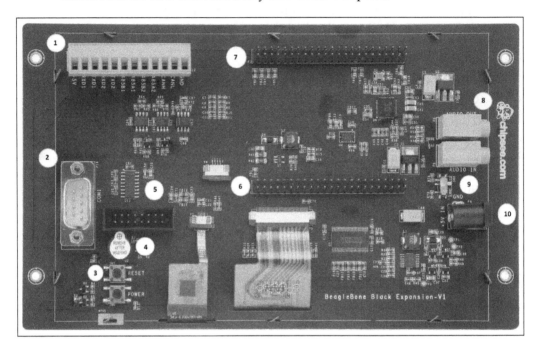

On the front side (from up to down), the board consists of the following:

- **5 programmable user's keys**: With Android, they are associated with the home screen and the back, menu, volume up, and volume down buttons

- **Blue LED**: This denotes CPU activity in the Android OS

- **Green LED**: This denotes power in the Android OS

# Installing a system for the expansion board

Chipsee provides different operating systems that you can install to start and manage the display. Having a look at these different OSes will help you to choose the one that will fit your project best.

## Looking at the available operating systems

Chipsee proposes a wide range of operating systems, which are provided in the following table:

| Operating system | Features | Comments |
| --- | --- | --- |
| Android | This is versatile and ergonomic and has a large market to offer | This is unsuitable for embedded boards' customization |
| Debian | This offers rich apps and is documented and open source | The provided version is more desktop- or server-oriented |
| TI Linux EZSDK | This is vastly documented, good for exploration and learning, and designed for embedded apps | This is not for beginners and has a non-negligible learning curve |

We will now look at how to install Android, Debian, and EZSDK and finally see how Android can be used for some multimedia experiences.

# Retrieving the latest files, images, documentation, or software

Even if you are provided with two CD-ROMs that include the documentation, user manual, and software, it's better to download the latest versions delivered by the manufacturer at `http://chipsee.eu/index.php?option=com_jdownloads&Itemi d=204&view=viewcategory&catid=18`.

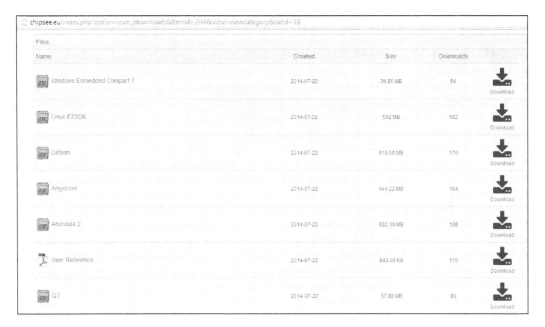

# Installing drivers

You can install Android USB drivers for the Windows platform. These drivers are located at `YourRoot:\Chipsee\Android4.2\Android4.2\SoftWare\Tools\usb_ driver`.

The installation is straightforward for any driver. You will end up with a new **Android phone** device. This way, you are able to use it as a disk.

# Prerequisites for installing any system

Before going into the OS installation, we have to check some things, such as the SD card naming, and we have to set the local language.

# Considering a virtual machine

All the following explanations are for installation from Linux as a native operating system. You can install directly on your computer or you can use a virtual machine as well. If you want to make some developments or try some different projects, a VM is the best solution. Similar to a Python virtual environment, which we have seen in *Chapter 4*, *Getting Your Own Video and Feeds*, virtual machines give you the freedom to experiment with everything you want without losing your system.

There are many free virtualization managers that you can install; these are the most famous ones:

- VirtualBox (`https://www.virtualbox.org/`): This is easy and fast to configure.

- VMware (player) (`http://www.vmware.com`): This is as easy as VirtualBox but has some limitations in the free version.

- QEMU (`www.qemu.org`): This is harder to configure than the two previous ones, but the only one that comes close to hardware emulation. This solution is recommended when you don't have your ARM board with you but still need to use it.

In addition, VirtualBox and QEMU are open source applications, so you will have additional tools proposed by their respective communities.

# Finding your SD card device

All the scripts provided are simple enough to require a single parameter: the SD card device's name. Let's see two ways to check the SD card device's name.

 You won't see the device until the SD card is effectively inserted, and not just the USB reader.

## Listing devices with lsblk

For example, after inserting an 8-GB SD card, we can use *lsblk*, a useful tool that is provided with our Linux distributions (`http://linux.die.net/man/8/lsblk`). The name stands for *list block devices*, so you have a tree of all the block devices that Linux is able to manage.

Just start *lsblk* from the command line, as shown here:

```
david@BBB-VM:~/bbb/Livre/Chipsee/Debian/Prebuilt/prebuilt-debian-bbb-exp-20140322 > lsblk
NAME    MAJ:MIN RM   SIZE RO TYPE MOUNTPOINT
sda      8:0     0    60G  0 disk
|-sda1   8:1     0  56.8G  0 part /
|-sda2   8:2     0    1K  0 part
`-sda5   8:5     0   3.3G  0 part [SWAP]
sdf      8:80    1   7.5G  0 disk
sr0     11:0     1  1024M  0 rom
```

Depending on the size we are looking for and the device type, we can deduce that our SD card is currently **sdf**.

## Using the dmesg utility

Remember in *Chapter 4*, *Getting Your Own Video and Feeds*, we looked into the system messages to find how our USB webcam was named. Here, we use the same recipe:

**dmesg | grep 'sd.'**

```
   8.598606] sd 2:0:0:4: Attached scsi generic sg6 type 0
   8.625231] sd 2:0:0:0: [sdb] Attached SCSI removable disk
   8.627034] sd 2:0:0:1: [sdc] Attached SCSI removable disk
   8.628905] sd 2:0:0:2: [sdd] Attached SCSI removable disk
   8.631028] sd 2:0:0:3: [sde] Attached SCSI removable disk
   8.631863] sd 2:0:0:4: [sdf] 15759360 512-byte logical blocks: (8.06 GB/7.51 GiB)
   8.636249] sd 2:0:0:4: [sdf] Write Protect is off
   8.636255] sd 2:0:0:4: [sdf] Mode Sense: 03 00 00 00
   8.641985] sd 2:0:0:4: [sdf] No Caching mode page found
   8.641991] sd 2:0:0:4: [sdf] Assuming drive cache: write through
   8.653663] sd 2:0:0:4: [sdf] No Caching mode page found
   8.653669] sd 2:0:0:4: [sdf] Assuming drive cache: write through
   8.657277]  sdf: unknown partition table
   8.669444] sd 2:0:0:4: [sdf] No Caching mode page found
   8.669450] sd 2:0:0:4: [sdf] Assuming drive cache: write through
   8.669455] sd 2:0:0:4: [sdf] Attached SCSI removable disk
  18.426876] Adding 3405820k swap on /dev/sda5.  Priority:-1 extents:1 across:3405820k FS
```

While being verbose, dmesg ensures that you format the correct device.

## Checking your investigation

In all cases, ensure that you are using the correct device to partition:

**fdisk -l /dev/sdf**

With a new card, this command should return the following line of code:

**/dev/sdf empty table partition**

# Adapting foreign systems for the installer script

If you execute the provided installation scripts from a non-English speaking system, you will end up with a nonbootable BeagleBone. This is because the installation scripts rely on text searches and matches. For example, in French, instead of the term "disk" and "cylinders," the results will be "disque" and "cylindres," respectively. These are results that the script doesn't understand, and in the end no system will be properly installed.

A simple workaround for Debian systems is to edit your locale file, as follows:

```
/etc/default/locale :
LANG="en_US"
LANGUAGE="en_US:en"
```

If, however, you'd like to keep the original language, then comment it with # at the beginning, use the script, and uncomment it thereafter.

Save the file and reboot to have the settings applied.

# Installing your system

Now, it's time to prepare the expansion board and to install an operating system. We'll go through the three main OSes; the processes for each one are similar. However, for beginners, we will describe which file to install.

# Installing and using Android

After you have downloaded the compressed Android file on your, you need to copy it to a dedicated directory. This is can be handy, so you can install all the three OSes beside each other in a separate space. So, if you are not really happy with Android, you can try Debian and get back to Android by a simple installation command.

Here's the procedure to do this, which is quite simple:

```
tar vzxf prebuilt-jb42-bbb-exp-20140321.tar.gz
cd prebuilt-jb42-bbb-exp-20140321
sudo fdisk -l /dev/sdf
sudo ./mksdcard.sh --device /dev/sdf
```

The 3rd part is just a check for you to be sure that you don't format your computer.

When installing Android, you need to validate the installation by pressing the Y key so that the installation process starts:

```
david@BBB-VM:~/bbb/Livre/Chipsee/prebuilt-jb42-bbb-exp-20140321 > sudo ./mkmmc-android.sh /dev/sdf
Assuming Default Locations for Prebuilt Images
All data on /dev/sdf now will be destroyed! Continue? [y/n]
y
[Unmounting all existing partitions on the device ]
umount: /dev/sdf: not mounted
umount: /dev/sdf1: not mounted
umount: /dev/sdf2: not mounted
[Partitioning /dev/sdf...]
Disk /dev/sdf doesn't contain a valid partition table
DISK SIZE - 8068792320 bytes
CYLINDERS - 980
[Making filesystems...]
[Copying files...]
[Extracting rootfs...]
[Extracting usrdata...]
```

Wait for the **Done** message, which notifies the end of the installation process. Plug your SD card into the BeagleBone board and power it on.

 Remember to press the user button to tell the board to start using SD not eMMC. This button is located on the other side of the SD card slot.

You will have to wait for a while for the boot to be achieved, which is particularly long for Android compared with the others. However, our comfort comes at this price, doesn't it?

If you want, go directly to a walkthrough with Android; skip the next parts until the *Using the expansion board with Android* section.

## Installing and using Debian

As we did for Android, you can define your boot disk with some easy steps (please remember that *sdf* is an example; you need to check your own SD card device's name):

```
tar vzxf prebuilt-debian-bbb-exp-20140322.tar.gz
cd Prebuilt/prebuilt-debian-bbb-exp-20140322
sudo fdisk -l /dev/sdf
sudo ./mksdcard.sh --device /dev/sdf
```

As for Android, when installing Debian, you are asked to validate your choice before you start the installation process, as shown in the following screenshot:

```
david@BBB-VM:~/bbb/Livre/Chipsee/Debian/Prebuilt/prebuilt-debian-bbb-exp-20140322 > sudo ./mksdcard.sh --device /dev/sdf
****************************************************
*                                                  *
*         THIS WILL DELETE ALL THE DATA ON /dev/sdf  *
*                                                  *
*      WARNING! Make sure your computer does not go  *
*               in to idle mode while this script is  *
*               running. The script will complete,   *
*               but your SD card may be corrupted.    *
*                                                  *
*         Press <ENTER> to confirm....             *
****************************************************
```

This will take a while; wait until the **Done** message appears.

The connection and usage is pretty straightforward; we find the system that we had in the previous chapters with MediaDrop. With Debian, you will have fewer things to learn and you can install it finally. When you think about which system to install, this is something for you to consider.

 All in all, a good idea can be to install MediaDrop and servers to the Debian OS with the Chipsee display, so you can have all the servers and a media player as well.

From SSH, the credentials to connect to the Debian OS are as follows:

- **User**: debian
- **Password**: chipsee

## Installing and using TI EZSDK

Texas Instruments is the manufacturer of the BeagleBone Black controller. Actually, they did a great job of giving exhaustive documentation and even their own version of Linux dedicated to this board. TI's version is for those who want to learn the hardware parts. Execute the following commands:

```
tar vzxf prebuilt-chipsee-bbb-exp-ezsdk-20131210.tar.gz
cd Linux-EZSDK/prebuilt
sudo fdisk -l /dev/sdf
sudo ./mksdcard.sh --device /dev/sdf
```

After the board is powered on with the user button, a nice Linux and TI's logo will make you wait for a bit to load the special environment called a **matrix**.

Here's a compilation of the main application spaces you will find in Matrix:

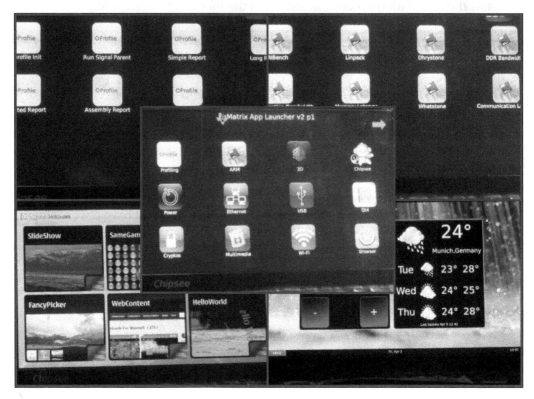

## Taking a look at TI's linux unique tools

After starting, you'll find the *app launcher*, a kind of desktop that centralizes all the available applications:

- **Profiling (up left)**: Examples for process, reports, and kernel profiling.
- **Benchmarking (up right)**: NBench (from the Byte magazine), linpack (single precision tests), Dhrystone, DDR, pipe communication's bandwidth, memory latency, Whetstone, latencies (fork, signals, TCP servicing, and so on).
- **Qt4/QML (down left)**: *Qt Quick Playground* which is great for the QML developers. In this group are many examples to test in this script language.
- **Qt4**: There are 3 demos *Animated Tiles*, *Thermostat Demo* (down right), and *Deform*.
- **Cryptos**: Examples for everything concerning cryptography from secure, server, to AES, SHA1, and OpenSSL benchmarking.
- **Multimedia**: Audio, MPEG4, and H264 decoding applications.

- **Power**: Set your CPU frequencies: 275 to 720 MHz, suspend/resume.
- There are more applications to explore, paying particular attention to settings/system *Shutdown,* which is handy to power off the system.

## TI's website

For the complete documentation and explanations about the SDK and information on the AM335x microcontroller, a good source will be `http://software-dl.ti.com/sitara_linux/esd/AM335xSDK/latest/index_FDS.html`.

I think `http://processors.wiki.ti.com/index.php/Sitara_AM335x_Portal` will be a good place to visit if you need to do the following:

- Get into the controllers' details
- Develop applications, as follows:
  - Bare metal look for the composer studio, which is a complete development environment
  - Linux
  - Android
  - Yocto

- Training lab materials
- Training slides

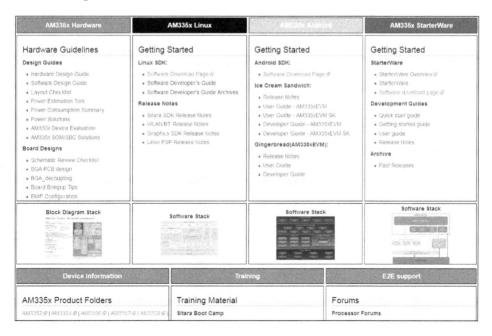

## Developing with Qt

TI' SDK is provided with a good amount of Qt sources and documentations.

If you take a look at the Qt archive, you'll see three documents, as shown here:

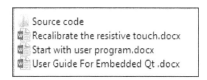

- **Start with the user program**: This is, in fact, a bash script that is worth taking a look at for GPIO usage

- **User Guide For Embedded Qt**: This shows you how to prepare, install, cross-compile, and get your application in the *Matrix* environment

- **Recalibrate the resistive touch**: This is the whole procedure for screen calibration

Aside is the `Example-applications.zip` file, which includes all the application sources you found in *Matrix*. These examples are for developers who already have a good technical background:

The `examples.tar.gz` file includes `demos` and `examples` that you find with all Qt installations, so they are all well-documented.

For more details about coding, these sources are strongly recommended.

# Using the expansion board with Android

With the installation completed, we will now use the expansion board as if it were a customized tablet.

## Using files from a computer

You have many options that you can use to exchange files, as follows:

- **USB devices**: Using the expansion board as a device, like a disk (see the *Installing drivers* section earlier in this chapter).

- **USB keys**: These can be used to get files from/to a computer and BeagleBone. The best way to have these recognized is to use the FAT32 filesystem. When the stick is plugged in, a styled Android logo appears, telling you that this new media is under analysis.

- Wi-Fi.

## Installing applications

You can install applications to the expansion board in many ways; here are a few examples:

- By manually copying the APK file to the SD card in the data directory and installing it from the provided Qt file explorer. Of course, this must be done offline.

- By downloading the APK file on the USB stick and installing it from the provided Qt file explorer.

- By browsing to the application's market website. This is the most handy way to have your application installed; however, this implies that you have Wi-Fi through a USB dongle and you have referenced your Google account in the settings panel.

For example, here is a screenshot that you would see during the *SSHDroid SSH* server installation:

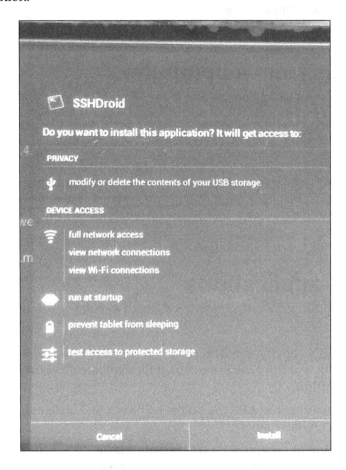

This little software is handy if you want to use the same SSH connection you had when communicating with Debian previously.

# Games

Of course, the Chipsee expansion board can also be used as a game console, thanks to the included accelerometer.

The prebuilt image includes many games you can play such as **NFS Shift**, A tilt **3D labyrinth**, **Angry birds**, **Fruit slice**, and more. Here's a compilation:

What is cool about this board is that the 3-axis accelerometer can be used for the games. However, before you do that, you need to configure it by performing the following steps:

1. Start **Chipsee Touch** to calibrate the screen.

2. Start **Chipsee sensor tool** to define the axis properly, as shown in the following screenshot:

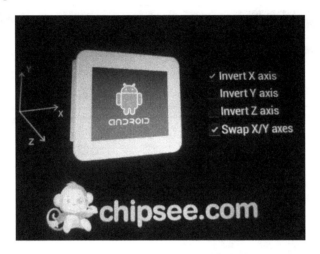

That way, the sensor will react properly with the board.

# Watching and listening to media

On the prebuilt image, you can find some demo videos. Notice that even if there is no hardware decoder, the board is totally able to render different video formats.

To watch to a video, click on the application's group icon and then select **Mobo Player**.

This application is a movie player and a picture viewer as well.

You can also enter into the SD card directory—`Qt file manager/Storage/
sdcard1/Video`—so you can play the samples provided with the prebuilt image,
as shown in the following screenshot:

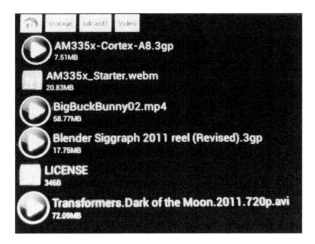

You can even play a video while doing something else. For this, while playing the
video, select the resize icon for the video's window to be resized to a smaller
dimension, as shown here:

# Summary

We addressed a topic that will be very useful for most of the media projects that you'll want to implement. The Chipsee expansion board lets you create an interactive object to watch videos, play some games, program in different languages, establish network and industrial communications, and many more.

What is important to note here is that this is a good platform for creative minds. It means that you can use these hardware capabilities for your own software, such as house management, media, server, and so on. In addition, I hope that you have now understood that the time you've spent to learn the command line and the Linux system from the previous chapters have been useful here. This knowledge can be reused for your next projects, embedded or not. This is the most important thing: to learn once and then deploy multiple times.

From the BeagleBone market place, the Chipsee expansion board is just one item among many capes; you should regularly visit the capes store for new boards. These choices let you have many different combinations to be experimented with. Imagine that we were playing with a single BeagleBone and now this configuration can be a part of a network of multiple BeagleBones, each one equipped with a different cape using sensors/actuators, thus allowing you to have wider projects.

We will now abandon the hardware part of this book and continue on our journey of creativity by taking a look at the software side of the journey in the same spirit. In the end, you can have your own software.

# 6
# Illuminate Your Imagination with Your Own Projects

The previous chapter showed that the BeagleBone Black board is designed to accept hardware add-ons called capes and how they ease the setup of projects. We can apply the same philosophy to the software part, thanks to the different tools that help developers. Now, in this chapter, we will go further with our hands-on approach by creating our applications.

You'll then have an overall view of how you can realize your own ideas without many difficulties. Thus the main purpose of this chapter could be resumed as:

> *Give a man a fish and you feed him for a day; teach a man to fish and you feed him for a lifetime*

I hope that you'll be more eager to develop projects by yourself afterwards.

In this chapter, we will cover the following topics:

- Presenting the "matrix revolution"
- Diving into the software parts
- Example 1 – our first client server application
- Example 2 – improving the first example by adding functionalities
- Example 3 – creating animated graphical patterns
- Final words

# Presenting the "matrix revolution"

This project aims to connect a matrix to the BeagleBone board so that it can be remotely accessed through a network connection. For this purpose, you will program the following parts:

- The client that will establish a connection to the server

- The server on the BeagleBone where you'll be able to interact with all the connected devices

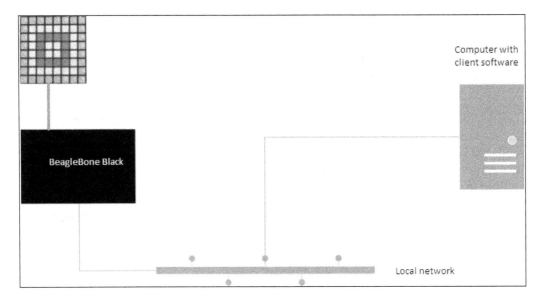

This project allows you to approach the following technologies:

- **BeagleBone/I2C**: This board communicates with the matrix using the I2C protocol (introduced later).

- **Adafruit matrix**: The matrix itself in the bicolor version. The good part is that when you buy two colors, you can have three (the combination of green with red will give you the orange color too).

- **Client**: Even though the hardware part will be the same among the different examples, you are going to implement different ways to control the matrix. These examples will then be different versions of a client program, which can run on a single PC, for example.

- **Server**: From the other side of the network, the BeagleBone board will have a dedicated program that will wait for commands to be executed. Similar to the client, this part will also evolve along with the project.

- **Python**: This is a well-known and widely-used language that lets you focus on the project quickly.

- **Code repository**: Writing code is an activity that lives, which moves as programs are not written in stone. This is why a companion repository for this book has been created on **GitHub**. With this online code base, you only need to retrieve the *Matrix Revolution* repository with the local git command. As you have already used Git in the previous chapters, you know that with a simple command you are sure to work with the last changes (corrections, improvements, fixes, and so on) from the author. The dedicated site can be found at http://dlewin.github.io/BeagleboneBlack-Server-Book, as shown in the following screenshot:

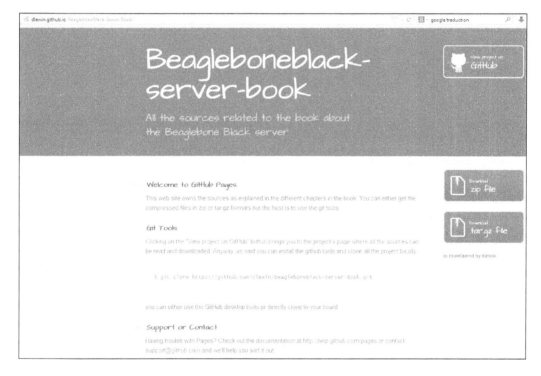

- This is the entry point, in the form of a website where you can grab the latest version of the projects as a compressed file and get basic details.

- ○ Accustomed coders will prefer a more detailed view with commit dates, information about which files have been pulled in the repository, and so on. Indeed, this other view of the site will let you walk through, read, or retrieve the code in many different ways.

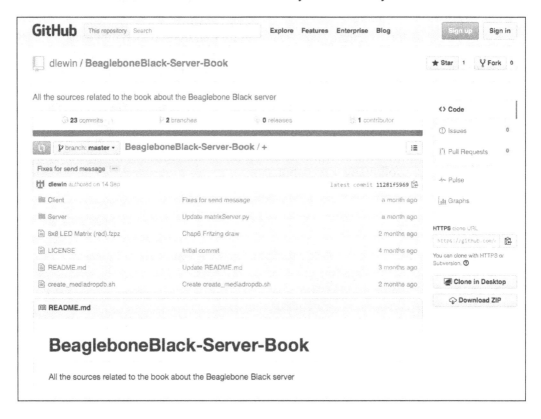

- ○ This being said, the best (and the only) way to get the code is to use `git` from the command line of your board:

```
git clone https://github.com/dlewin/BeagleboneBlack-Server-
Book.git
```

Now that you know what you are going to play with, we'll mix these technologies in three flavors, elaborating in a progressive manner. Obviously, this implies that you need some additional knowledge but rest assured that it will be explained sufficiently. Having said that, you need to be at ease with the example and its concepts before you go to the next step.

# The LED matrix

The graphical representation of this project will be a matrix of LEDs that Adafruit has arranged in a very handy product, and there is no need to for additional components such as resistors, power circuits, and so on: the box contains all that is required to start quickly.

You can get more details from their website at `http://www.adafruit.com/products/902`.

When you receive it, you just need to solder some pins as indicated in the Adafruit documentation and it's ready to be used. As shown in the presentation, the messages between the matrix and the BeagleBone Black board use a form of the I2C protocol. Let's look how it works.

# Introducing I2C

Whichever board you use in your projects—Arduino, Raspberry, Mini2440—most of the time, you need to deal with sensors, components, or devices that "talk" I2C or SPI. These data buses simplify our coder's life. Indeed, our matrix just need to be managed with only two signals, *SCL* and *DAT*, to execute all the operations.

Instead of a wire for each function, a communication is specified by Philips on the two wires with the *protocol* part of the I2C. Fortunately, this happens behind the scenes, thanks to the I2C Linux driver.

 Are you interested in getting more details about the I2C bus? Check out `http://support.saleae.com/hc/en-us/articles/200730905-Learn-I2C-Inter-Integrated-Circuit` for an interesting explanation.

Using the driver means that, even though you use the I2C protocol, you never have to deal with the bus message frames, CRC, and all the detail of the protocol, so you can focus on the data to be sent from BeagleBone to the matrix.

# Wiring the matrix to the board

After this short introduction to the I2C protocol, we can now set up the connection between the two devices, as shown here:

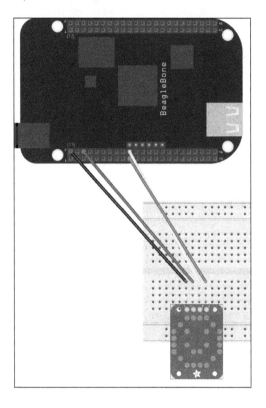

 This image is not a drawing. You can obtain the source file from the GitHub website as a design file in order to use it with **Fritzing** (http://fritzing.org/home/), an open source electronic design software.

Assuming that the matrix is now built, we can wire the matrix according to the following schema:

- **SCL**: Pin 20
- **DAT**: Pin 19
- **+5V**: Pin 6
- **GND**: Pin 2

Instead of 5V, you can use the 3.3V power as well, but this will result in less brightness.

The synoptic is easy to understand: just wire the four pins to the board. However after this, if you want to access the complete header's reference, check the header documentation provided by the BeagleBone Wiki at `http://elinux.org/ Beagleboard:Cape_Expansion_Headers`.

| P9 | | | |
|---|---|---|---|
| DGND | 1 | 2 | DGND |
| VDD_3V3 | 3 | 4 | VDD_3V3 |
| VDD_5V | 5 | 6 | VDD_5V |
| SYS_5V | 7 | 8 | SYS_5V |
| PWR_BUT | 9 | 10 | SYS_RESETN |
| GPIO_30 | 11 | 12 | GPIO_60 |
| GPIO_31 | 13 | 14 | GPIO_40 |
| GPIO_48 | 15 | 16 | GPIO_51 |
| I2C1_SCL | 17 | 18 | I2C1_SDA |
| I2C2_SCL | 19 | 20 | I2C2_SDA |
| I2C2_SCL | 21 | 22 | I2C2_SDA |
| GPIO_49 | 23 | 24 | I2C1_SCL |
| GPIO_117 | 25 | 26 | I2C1_SDA |
| GPIO_125 | 27 | 28 | GPIO_123 |
| GPIO_121 | 29 | 30 | GPIO_122 |
| GPIO_120 | 31 | 32 | VDD_ADC |
| AIN4 | 33 | 34 | GNDA_ADC |
| AIN6 | 35 | 36 | AIN5 |
| AIN2 | 37 | 38 | AIN3 |
| AIN0 | 39 | 40 | AIN1 |
| GPIO_20 | 41 | 42 | GPIO_7 |
| DGND | 43 | 44 | DGND |
| DGND | 45 | 46 | DGND |

For our experiments, we use the I2C-2 because the device's tree file defines that the I2C-1 is already used.

Usually, you should ensure that the function pin you intend to use is free.

 This subject is outside the scope of this book and requires you to understand the device tree mechanism. A complete explanation can be found in the Free Electron presentation at `http:// free-electrons.com/pub/conferences/2013/elce/ petazzoni-device-tree-dummies/petazzoni-device- tree-dummies.pdf`.

As BeagleBone Black was the first to follow the recommended guidelines, our board is used as an example along with the explanation, which is handy.

# Diving into the software

We have set up the hardware that will be used along this chapter. Now, let's develop our application to give it some life.

# Example 1 – our first client server application

Assuming that you retrieved the whole project in your local directory, simply go to the `server_1` directory and open `matrixServer.py`.

## Installing the requirements

Looking at the code parts, some prerequisites must be followed for both the server and client sides.

For the server, you can use the following command:

```
sudo pip install twisted
```

Alternatively, you can use the following line:

```
Install python-twisted
```

For the client part, you'll need to install the Python environment according to your operating system from `https://www.python.org/downloads/`.

The code that we'll use here is compatible with both the 2.7 and 3 versions.

Additionally, you'll need a *twisted matrix*, which you can retrieve with this command:

```
pip install twisted
```

Alternatively, you can obtain the one for your operating system from `https://twistedmatrix.com/trac/wiki/Downloads`.

The hardware is set up and the requirements are in place; you are ready to run the example.

# Running the example

Server_3/matrixServer.py                                    Client/client3/

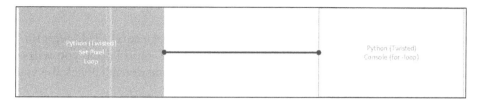

Connect to the BeagleBone Black board with PuTTY or any SSH client and enter in the directory, as indicated:

`debian@arm:~/BeagleboneBlack-Server-Book/Server/Server_1$ ./matrixServer.py`

```
debian@arm:~/BeagleboneBlack-Server-Book/Server/Server_1$ ./matrixServer.py
 Running the server on port 8000
```

The message shown in the preceding screenshot indicates that the server is running correctly and is now waiting to accept a client connection. However, if you don't run the server before the client, you'll end up with the following message:

`>>>`
`Connection failed - goodbye!`

As soon as you start the client after the server, the client immediately loops over the data and you can see that the matrix gets its LEDs in green, according to that loop:

```
debian@arm:~/BeagleboneBlack-Server-Book/Server/Server_1$ ./matrixServer.py
 Running the server on port 8000
0 0
0 1
0 2
0 3
0 4
0 5
0 6
0 7
1 0
1 1
1 2
1 3
1 4
1 5
1 6
1 7
```

On the server display (the SSH connection), you can also check the coordinates for the LED that is currently set.

# Jumping into the code

When it is running on BeagleBone, the unique purpose of a server is to wait for the incoming data. If you intend to modify the server's code — and I hope you will — be warned that in order to keep the example simple, the code doesn't check the viability of the data sent from the client.

# Description of the data packet

Each time the server receives data, it will look for the following three values:

- The X position
- The Y position
- Color

If you want to expand this format, you'll need to apply modifications on both the server and client sides.

# Describing the server code

As soon as the server receives a data packet, it will transcode it into I2C, then be able to address each LED individually.

So, functionally speaking, the server can be seen as a "remote and translator" between the client application and each LED.

Now, let's dive into the main parts of the source:

```
import sys
sys.path.append('..')                        # Adafruit libs are in previous dir

from Adafruit_8x8 import ColorEightByEight
from twisted.internet import reactor, protocol
import time
```

The preceding lines of code state that the required libraries (that is, Adafruit) are not in the standard path, but they can be found in the directory upwards. That way, if a new version is available, you just have to retrieve it (git pull), and you won't have to copy/paste into directories, as it's made transparent to you.

The code uses a modified version of the Adafruit library, which has some fixes. So, as long as you are using the bicolor version of the matrix, you should use this library only.

```
grid = ColorEightByEight(address=0x70)
```

The grid-based object needs to be instantiated in the program with an identified address, 0x70.

 Here's a tip about I2C-tools: If you want to know where this address comes from, watch the video at http://derekmolloy. ie/beaglebone/beaglebone-an-i2c-tutorial- interfacing-to-a-bma180-accelerometer/.

The remaining code is taken from the *twisted matrix* examples, which are handy to manage network applications. Finally, the following screenshot shows the main part of the server code:

```
class EchoClient(protocol.Protocol):
    """Once connected, send a message, then print the result."""

    def connectionMade(self):
        for i in range(0,8):
            for j in range(0,8):
                conct = str(i) + str(j) + str(1)
                #self.transport.write(conct +'\r\n')
                self.transport.write(conct)
                print conct
```

The client part is also based on the *Twisted Matrix* example with a modification in the EchoClient class. The client will do the following:

- Establish a connection to the server.

- Check whether the server is alive.

- With a successful connection, some frames are generated to fill the matrix line by line. This is the purpose of the two for loops.

When the client has finished, the matrix appears with all its LEDs lit, as shown here:

What we have done so far is connecting our client application to a specific server in order to provide a service—remember the translation we talked about before—dedicated to a device, which is our LED matrix.

From a larger point of view, we have seen a project that aims to implement some customized hardware.

You can easily adapt this project to use any hardware of your choice or any off-the-shelf modules available, as described in the cape paragraph from *Chapter 5, Building Your Media Player*.

## Questions and suggestions related to this example

The following are the questions and suggestions related to this example:

- Have you noticed that with the provided library the loop evolves in a particular sense?

- I've left a `clear_matrix` function that is yet to be used: what needs to be implemented on the client side in order to request the matrix to be cleared?

- You can imagine action words to create your own protocol, such as executing a predefined pattern, animation, and so on.

- Instead of using a hardcoded configuration, a cool improvement will be to parse an external file. For example, you can use `configparser` (`https://wiki.python.org/moin/ConfigParserExamples`), or if you don't like INI files, the **PyYAML** syntax (`http://pyyaml.org/wiki/PyYAML`) is a good alternative.

# Example 2 – improving the first example by adding functionalities

As you have quickly acquired confidence with the previous example, I'm sure you want to improve your project, and different ideas might come to mind. We are going to implement some of them.

# From the client side

Based on the previous client-server scenario, it will be handy to add a graphical interface to the client in order to visually control the matrix. The GUI must be able to run on most known platforms, smartphones included.

We also want to control each LED color from the client side. Obviously, using all the available LED colors is now required, so we will add a dedicated control to the interface for this purpose.

# From the server side

In the previous example, our focus was on the basic concepts to validate the project; we now intend to improve it. On the other side, the main evolution of the server is to find a way to allow each LED to evolve one after the other in a "traditional" direction, that is, from the top-left to bottom-right.

Actually, this is not exactly true. If you take a look at the provided code, you can see that some more functionality has already been implemented, but we will see this at the end of this second part:

Server_2/matrixServer.py                    Client/client2.py

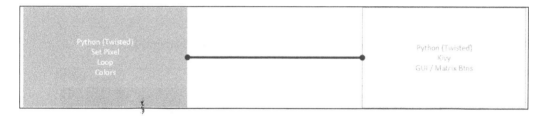

# Improving the client with Kivy

Using the Python language, **Kivy** is an open source library that can be used to code graphical interfaces easily. With Kivy, you can run your project's executable on many targets, such as Windows, Linux, OS X, Android, and iOS. Multitouch is something that is also possible.

You can obtain Kivy for different platforms from `http://kivy.org/#download`.

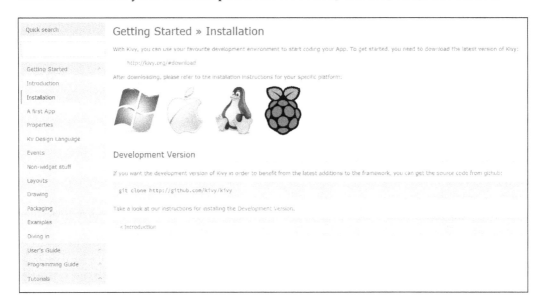

Please follow the installation guidelines (`http://kivy.org/docs/installation/installation-windows.html` for Windows users) in order to be able to use the following example.

The following screenshot shows how this second version is organized:

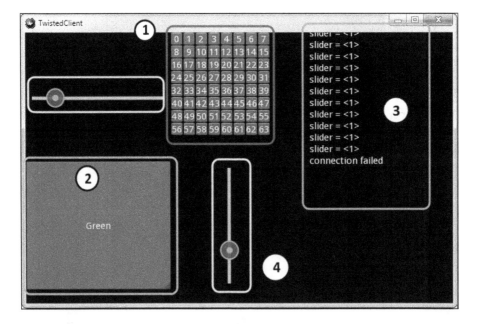

This application aims to be seen as a laboratory where you can have different experiments; therefore, no effort is put into the presentation, in order to focus on code simplicity for better understanding. Our laboratory is composed of the controls we spoke about in the improvements. Those controls can be split into four main groups, as follows:

- 64 buttons organized in a matrix, representing each LED individually. Each time you click on any button, you will see the corresponding LED lit on the matrix.

- A list of choices to select the color before you click on the matrix button.

- A log where you can see events, such as the current connection status of the board, some values, debugging information, and so on.

- Some additional splitters, which are kept for the last part of this example.

Sharing the same code as the previous example, this client comes with additional functionality anyway. Let's take a look at the code; it is shown in the following screenshot:

```python
class TwistedClientApp(App):
    connection = None

    def build(self):
        root = self.setup_gui()
        self.connect_to_server()
        return root
```

The `build` method from `TwistedClientApp` is called to execute `setup_gui` and `connect_to_server`.

Thus, the `Setup_gui` method is the main method used to set up the interface, as shown here:

```python
def setup_gui(self):
    self.ParentLayout = GridLayout(cols=3, row_force_default=True, row_default_height=200)
    self.label = Label(text='connecting...\n')

    # Additional code to exercise, so you can adapt related code on server for example
    Matrix_Row_Slider = Slider(min=0, max=8, value=1)
    Matrix_Row_Slider.bind(value=self.onMatrix_Row_Slidervalue)  # handy to know what are the slider's position

    Matrix_Col_Slider = Slider(min=0, max=8, value=1)
    Matrix_Col_Slider = Slider(orientation='vertical')

    self.ParentLayout.add_widget(Matrix_Row_Slider)
    self.Matrix_Layout = GridLayout(cols=8)

    # Let's add a spinner to be able to select some colors
    self.Colorspinner = Spinner(text='Green', values=('NA','Green','Red','Orange', 'Cls'), size_hint=(None, None))

    # We define the main buttons matrix here
    for i in range(64):
        btn = Button(text=str(i), size_hint_x=None,size_hint_y=None, width=20, height=20 )
        btn.bind(on_press=self.callback)
        self.Matrix_Layout.add_widget(btn)

    self.ParentLayout.add_widget(self.Matrix_Layout)
    self.ParentLayout.add_widget(self.label)
    self.ParentLayout.add_widget(self.Colorspinner)
    self.ParentLayout.add_widget(Matrix_Col_Slider)
    return self.ParentLayout
```

**(1)** **(2)** **(3)** **(4)**

This is where you define which controls will be inserted and their arrangement, and more precisely their layout:

1.  **Label**: As we want to define our GUI on three different parts of the screen, the program relies on a grid *layout*. The method also defines a text zone dedicated to the communications with the board, debugging details, and so on.

2.  **Spinner**: This is a color selector when clicked on so that you can choose a color.

3.  **A matrix made up of 64 buttons**: Instead of defining all of them individually, a `for` loop is in charge of instantiating all the buttons. We then associate (*bind*) each new button click event to a dedicated handler (*callback*). Let's take a look at this callback method; it is shown in the following screenshot:

```
def callback(self,instance):
    self.print_message('Button nb <%s> pressed' % instance.text)
    Btn_nb = int(instance.text)
    Btn_x= Btn_nb %8
    Btn_y= int((Btn_nb  ) / 8)
    self.print_message('x <%d> ' %Btn_x )
    self.print_message('y <%d> ' %Btn_y )

    SpinValue = self.Colorspinner.values.index(self.Colorspinner.text)
    if SpinValue:
        Color = SpinValue
    else:
        Color=str(1)
    self.print_message('Color <%s> ' % Color)

    Conct = str(Btn_x) + str(Btn_y)+ str(Color)
    self.send_message(Conct)
```

4. **Layout management**: We insert different controls in our grid layout, knowing that the order is important.

Each time a button is clicked, the related callback will be called. Then, in the callback, we can handle the event by doing some computations and eventually print out some text about which button has been pressed to the log window next to it.

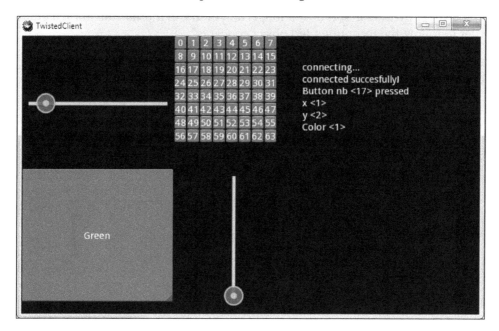

After playing along with the client, you can see your requests executed on the matrix and then some LEDS set with different colors, as shown in the following screenshot:

## Questions and thoughts related to this example

The Setup_Gui method is somewhat long; can you try to modify the implementation in order to follow the recommended object concepts?

It won't take much time to change the callback so that it can handle colors without selecting them from the list. Here's a hint: you can get inspired from the next example.

If you have taken a closer look at the client code, you might see that some elements are waiting to be used and some others are left for improvement. For example, while two sliders are present, only one slider is able to display values. Both are left for improvement, so you can use them for whatever you want.

The same applies to the server code; we didn't use the Bargraph code at all.

[  *Sliders* and *Bargraphs* may be functionally relied. ]

# Example 3 – creating animated graphical patterns

The previous two examples focused on experimentation, hardware understanding, and communication above others. That having been acquired, with the third example we will keep the same client/server basis, while we will leave the laboratory concept to set up a more realistic project. By doing this, we will be coding an application that will have a better ergonomy with a finest aspect.

## Following the project's requirements

To achieve this goal, we are going to change the client programing language to use C++ with the Qt framework. Even though the example is quite simple, you'll need some C++ and object-oriented programming (OOP) knowledge. Qt is a framework that will allow you to keep the code universality, as in the previous example with Kivy, with a wider range of targets. As there are many similarities, you can then legitimately ask yourself why you need to change all the code? In this case, Qt benefits from many years of research and community efforts. Moreover and mostly, Qt provides more than GUI programming capabilities. Indeed, this vast and polyvalent framework gives access to various mechanisms for networks, threads, state machines, process communication, and so much more.

For installation purposes, you need to retrieve the proper installer from the download URL at http://qt-project.org/downloads.

Along with this installer, an editor is also provided, so you can start coding/compiling right away.

 After installation, to check your environment you can open QtCreator and start an empty **Qt Widgets Application** project. Compile it with the green triangle button on the left-hand side. As soon as you see a new empty application window popping up, this means that the compiler, the Qt Framework, and your settings are valid.

From now on, we will rely on QtCreator as the development environment. For the sake of everybody's spirit, everything is available from this environment. No external tools will be needed.

# Where to find help on the Internet

If you intend to develop projects but are afraid of C++ or Qt, then the Voidrealms website (http://www.voidrealms.com) is the solution for you.

There, the author has covered the most important subjects. From the very basic *hello world* to some advanced ones such as mutable, *Model-View-Delegate*, or *QtConcurrent*, you'll never waste a minute you spend there.

Indeed, behind the subjects that Voidrealms can explain, the concept is really attractive. Each topic is accompanied by a short video that allows you to get all the explanations, to finish each time with a single executable to understand and reproduce. The advantage of the video is that it has detailed explanations, and what is interesting is the mistakes that one can commit.

With most of the tutorials, you will also have a ZIP file of all the project sources of the video.

 Bryan is the only guy to give life to all of these tutorials; you might consider a donation if you find the site useful.

For those who already have some C++ skills and want to jump directly to Qt without an introduction, I've provided here the main topics that you'll find in our project:

- C++ Qt 04 - Signals and Slots
- C++ Qt 09 - QGridLayout
- C++ Qt 12 - QFile
- C++ Qt 13 - Resource Files
- C++ Qt 15 - QPushButton
- C++ Qt 36 - Introducing containers and the QList
- C++ Qt 63 - Introduction to Network Programming Concepts
- C++ Qt 65 - QTcpSocket basics

# Looking at the differences from the previous example

The previous example not only relies on the object programming paradigm but also on the way the information is represented. Indeed, while we will talk with the BeagleBone Black server in the same way, we'll configure the matrix on the computer with a totally different point of view by defining a more ergonomic GUI.

*Server_3/matrixServer.py*                                      *Client/Qt/Led_Matrix*

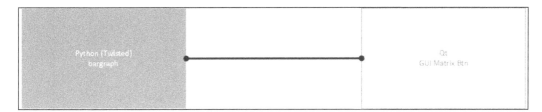

As we did in the previous chapters, let's list what is done in this third example, knowing that a pattern represents the status of all the LEDs in the matrix:

- The graphical interface reuses the matrix representation as shown previously but in a way that can be adapted to different square matrices. This is handy for anyone who needs to implement a matrix with a different size and a few modifications.

- The client is completely rewritten in **C++** and uses Qt.

- Each LED's status and color is set directly by a single click of the button. This allows you to define a pattern with different colors quickly.

- When you think that your pattern is complete, you have the possibility of saving it into a file or sending it directly.

- You can remove a pattern from the list.

- There is, of course, the possibility of loading some patterns from a file.

# Looking at the concepts of the matrix edition

From the previous paragraph, you might want to know how these new functionalities will interact together. The following schema should represent the main idea:

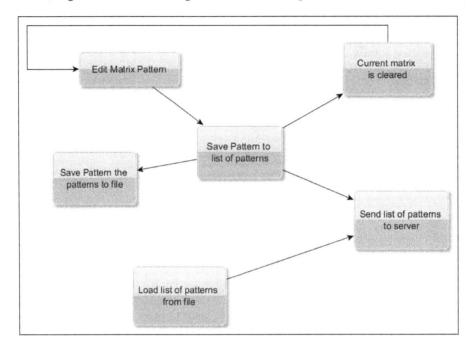

- Begin by editing your new pattern and validate it by saving it
- This allows you to keep it in the list of all the patterns at the same time
- Then you can send it to the BeagleBone server with the server code running
- Alternatively, you can also save the pattern to a file
- You can start the application by directly loading some previously saved patterns as well

# Browsing the code

As you have previously cloned the repository, the related Qt code is already in your hands and you simply need to change the directory from `Client2` to `Client/Qt`. Then perform the following steps:

1. In the new directory, you should see a bunch of CPP and HPP files.
2. Now, launch QtCreator and, from the **File** menu, select the **Open File or Project** submenu.

3. From the file's dialog box, select the `Led_Matrix.pro` file from the directory you found in step 1.

> If you remember, we previously stated that the code is a living thing, so checking the code base from time to time is a good habit:
>
> `Git pull`

# Compilation time

In the opened project, you can have a look at the code, compile it, and eventually modify it as well.

For now, we just compile it by clicking on the green triangle on the bottom-left.

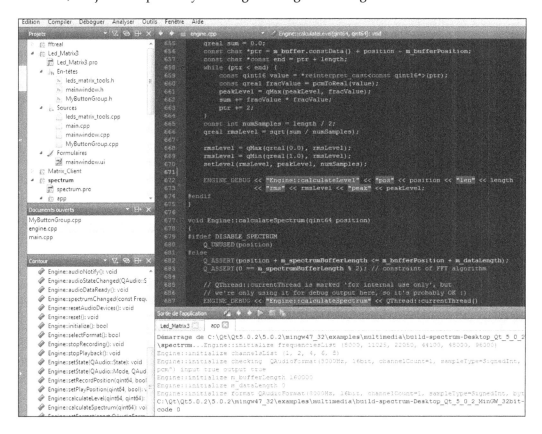

During the compilation, the output window displays some hints about eventual errors and warnings. On a successful build, the `leds_matrix` executable is displayed here:

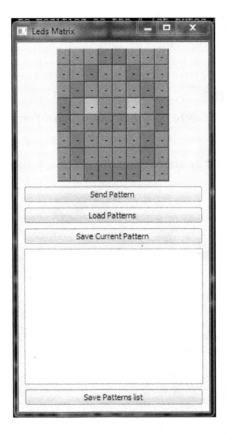

 The source code should be flexible enough so that if you want to draw a matrix with a different size, you won't have to make much modification to the code.

Of course, you won't have a drawing like this one at the start. You need to load your `Load patterns` file to start sending your patterns.

## Describing the GUI

You can now see how the `Led_Matrix` **Qt** application differs from the **Kivy** version.

The same matrix representation is used to let you design your pattern in the same way as before. However, an improvement has been made, as you don't have to select the color each time you click on a cell.

Indeed, the click follows a color cycle, as shown here:

Off -> Green -> Orange -> Red

This circular cycle ensures that the button is in the Off state again after the color Red. As soon as you are happy with your pattern, save it.

This adds your creation to the *patterns list*. Let's just use this single pattern for the moment.

 There is a difference between the two buttons that let you save patterns. While the **Save current pattern** button allows you to keep the current pattern in a list, the **Save patterns list** button will save all the patterns from the list into a file.

Now, click on **Send pattern**, which will read your pattern from the list and send it to the server. You should now see your matrix from the server cloning the pattern defined in the client, as shown in the following screenshot:

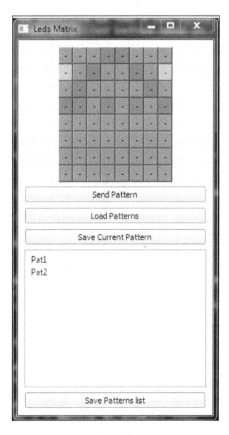

Obviously, the fun lies in defining different patterns to send to the matrix in order to end up with a cool animation. Don't hesitate to share your patterns by proposing them in the repository.

# A quick tour of the code

With this third example, I'd like to introduce you to a different approach for coding. The starting point is the main where an instance is created. The project is coded along two different classes:

- **MyButtonGroup**: This is dedicated to the graphical representation of the matrix (as opposed to the mathematical matrix)

- **Leds_Matrix_Tools**: This contains all the functions related to the matrix, writing the matrix, files operations, and so on

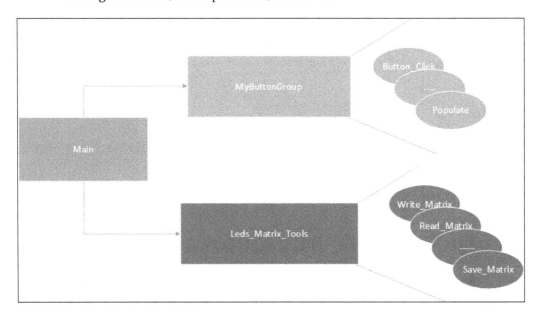

Adding code for 64 items individually is not viable; the object paradigm is done to avoid it. Thus, we don't have to create, instantiate, and code an event for each LED one by one in the graphical matrix. This is why MyButtonGroup was derived from the original QButtonGroup class.

Then, each item in the matrix has a SIGNAL/SLOT connection:

```
connect(this,SIGNAL(buttonClicked(QAbstractButton*)),
this, SLOT(buttonClick(QAbstractButton*)));
```

This helps us to create a dedicated event, as shown in the following screenshot:

```
void MyButtonGroup::buttonClick(QAbstractButton* button)
{
    int new_ID = abs (this->id(button)) -2              ;   // Adaptation to compute the btn

    unsigned short row = new_ID/8                       ;
    unsigned short col = new_ID - (8 * row)             ;

    unsigned short btn_value = this->Read_Matrix(row, col)  ;

    switch( btn_value )
    {
      case 0:    button->setStyleSheet("background-color:green;")   ;
        btn_value++
        break
      case 1:    button->setStyleSheet("background-color:orange;")  ;
        btn_value++
        break
      case 2:    button->setStyleSheet("background-color:red;")     ;
        btn_value++
        break
      case 3:    button->setStyleSheet("background-color:grey;")    ;
        btn_value = 0
        break
    }
    this->Write_Matrix(row, col,btn_value );
}
```

We are now free to add anything we want in the `ButtonClick` event handler. Therefore, this is the place to compute a button's position according to the `*button` pointer that is given as a call parameter.

However, this is not enough. The graphical buttons matrix has been separated from its logical representation. This is the role of the following command:

```
QStringList Leds_Matrix     ;
```

This aims to define a list of matrices. In addition, the idea is to use the functions provided with this container class—reverting, searching, removing, finding the first, last, and so on—so that you can create your own graphical algorithms in an easier way.

Some transformations within `switch` are done because even though we know which button has been clicked, we still ignore its position in the matrix. After this small calculation, it's easy to affect the buttons due to the color-changing cycle. By the way, we also update the logical matrix data.

# Looking at the main functions

Here is an overview of the other main functions:

- `Clear()`: This aims to empty the current pattern in the patterns list. This is used when `Leds_Matrix` needs to be reset from the constructor mainly.

- `Savefile_click()`: This is an event handler relied to the `Save_To_File` method, which will parse all the patterns and save them to the local file.

- `Save_To_File(QString Filename)`: This parses `patterns_list` to save all the patterns in the list into a local file.

- `Loadfile_click()`: This is an event handler relied to the `Load_From_File` method.

- `Load_From_File(QString Filename)`: This parses the local file to retrieve all the saved patterns in order to restore the patterns list.

- `Populate(QGridLayout *layout, MyButtonGroup* group )`: This is called only once, at the beginning of the application in order to initiate the graphical matrix.

- `Read_Matrix(unsigned short x)`: This a low-level function that takes a row/column and returns the color value found at these coordinates.

- `Write_Matrix(unsigned short x, unsigned short y, unsigned short value)`: This a low-level function that takes a row/column to write the color value at these coordinates.

- `Save_Pattern_click()`: This will walk through all the patterns loaded in memory and send them to the server. A small conversion is needed here to transform an array-like data into our three-data protocol (x, y, and color).

# Questions and thoughts related to this example

The questions and thoughts related to this example are given as follows:

- Did you notice that while the server is developed in Python, the C++ client can communicate with it. How is this possible?

- Try to find the limitations of this approach.

- What will you do if you intend to modify the time delay of the animation? Try to identify the part of the code related to this functionality.

- Will you apply this change in the client or from the server code?

- It's legitimate to question yourself when you intend to develop a new functionality in your project. Take a moment to compare both the client and server sides, as they each have their pros and cons.

# Summary

This last chapter helped us develop a complete client/server project. Throughout the book, you learned about the background information needed to install, configure, and deploy a client/server.

The main objective of this book being to let you create your own project; thus, we've addressed the hardware and software aspects of various projects. The integration of both sides is what makes embedded systems unique.

### Some final words

You can act on the code we saw here. These are not just words; you can be a part of this project by improving it. Here's how: when you think your modifications are good enough, send a change request to the *GitHub BeagleBone Black book* project and, after validation, you'll see your code included in the official repository.

# A
# Troubleshooting and Tricks to Improve Your Server

You can have the best book in your hands, but experimentation will always remain the best way to learn. It is even more true that, even after following the instructions provided in this book, you might experience some problems. Therefore, as nothing is written in stone, here you will find some topics to help you resolve different cases that can happen. From tricks to ease your life to troubleshooting steps, I have grouped the useful tools that you can implement daily.

In this chapter, we will cover the following situations:

- How to ease your life with the command line?
- When you need to retrieve open ports

## Ease your life with the command line

At the beginning, the command line can be confusing. Even though the instructions in the chapters of this book have been written for you to install in the easiest way, there's no reason to spend more time than necessary with this command line. Therefore, it's always helpful to have some tools and customizations on your system. In the long run, you will see that you will not be able to do without them.

## Package management

Throughout the chapters in this book, the Linux distribution package tools are never mentioned. Indeed, you will always have commands as follows:

```
install apackage
```

This intentional abstraction helps you focus on installation itself and is short, to keep you away from syntax errors. Most importantly, with this you can set up your commands toolbox in such a way that whenever you would want to change to a different distribution, you will still use `install package`. Here is how you can do this:

Go and edit your `bashrc` in the following directory:

`~/.bashrc`

Here, define some aliases for debian:

- `alias install="sudo apt-get install"`
- `alias update="sudo apt-get update"`
- `alias search="sudo apt-cache search"`

After saving and quitting the editor, you can apply your configuration using the following command:

`debian@beaglebone:~$ source ~/.bashrc`

As easy as it can be, you will then just rely on these commands most of the time to handle your system. In the case, when you use a different package system, you'll just have to modify accordingly, such as with Fedora:

- `alias install="yum install"`
- `alias update="yum update"`
- `alias search="yum list"`

# Get to know what you did previously

Let's keep on personalizing the `bashrc` file, but this time with the goal being to look backward for commands that you have already performed.

The aim of this trick is to avoid retyping the same command multiple times. Moreover, sometimes it's useful to analyze in which order you have executed different commands, one after the other. This is often the root cause of errors. This is where `histogrep` will make your life easier:

```
function histogrep{
history | grep $1
}
```

Source the file as in the previous topic, and try to search, a command you entered previously:

```
debian@beaglebone:~$ histogrep Mediadrop
```

# Different ways to find your files

When you don't remember where a specific file is located, you can rely on some Linux tools. In this specific case, let's say that we want to retrieve the deployment.ini location; thus we can use two different commands:

To find your files, run the following command:

```
(mediacore_env)debian@beaglebone:~$ find / -name production.ini -type f
2>/dev/null
```

The various parameters involved are as follows:

- / : We want to look into the root partition. Obviously, if you install MediaDrop to another partition, set it accordingly.
- -type f (optional): This optimizes the search, as we want to find only files but not directories.
- 2>/dev/null (optional): This is to remove annoying and most of the time useless *Permission denied* messages.

*While being really powerful, the* find *command requires some options, which you have to know, to use it well. The* locate *command is a quick and an easy way to find your file. You will have to install it, as this command is not installed, by default. You will retrieve it from the* mlocate *package.*

To request an update of the index of all your files, use the following command:

```
debian@beaglebone:~$ sudo updatedb
```

Now you can search for any file with the following command:

```
debian@beaglebone:~$ Locate production.ini
```

You have the result(s) instantly, faster than with the find command.

What is perturbing with locate is that you might not find a file that can exist anyway. This situation happens when the searched-for file had been created after the indexation of the locate database.

Each command has its own pros and cons; `find` is really handy and powerful but requires a lot of options that you need to know; on the other hand, `locate` is easy, and simple but requires being updated regularly.

# All you need to know about open network ports

As long as you aim at using BeagleBone Black for server purposes, many ports are going to be used. You will soon need to know those that are already assigned. For example, ports 8080 and 8000 are very often required so they will be most probably defined in many default configuration files when you install an application. Then, to avoid port conflicts, you will want to retrieve those that are currently used. For this, enter the following command:

```
debian@arm:~$ sudo netstat -an | grep LISTEN | grep -v ^unix

tcp       0      0 0.0.0.0:1984          0.0.0.0:*
LISTEN
tcp       0      0 127.0.0.1:3306        0.0.0.0:*
LISTEN
tcp       0      0 127.0.0.1:11211       0.0.0.0:*
LISTEN
tcp       0      0 0.0.0.0:22            0.0.0.0:*
LISTEN
tcp6      0      0 :::6600              :::*
LISTEN
tcp6      0      0 :::80                :::*
LISTEN
tcp6      0      0 :::22                :::*
LISTEN
```

In the beginning of this appendix, we have seen how to ease our life with aliases and functions.

I strongly suggest that you use the same technique with this long command. Thereafter, you won't hesitate any more to use it because you won't need to remember the whole syntax.

# Ideas to Improve Your Server

I think you have now understood the main value added by this book, which can be assumed to be "do more by yourself." Then, as a bonus, I thought you might be interested in some additional software.

As we mainly focused on servers for managing video files and streams, we'll see their musical equivalents, which are the following:

- MiniDLNA
- Subsonic

If you have read the chapters carefully and have successfully installed, configured, and run the software, then this appendix will bring you additional fun. Frankly speaking, you should be able to install these servers to your BeagleBone Black easily. Think of adding these extras servers as adding chocolate chunks to a cookie.

# MiniDLNA

Before we talk about the software that uses DLNA, let's first understand what it is.

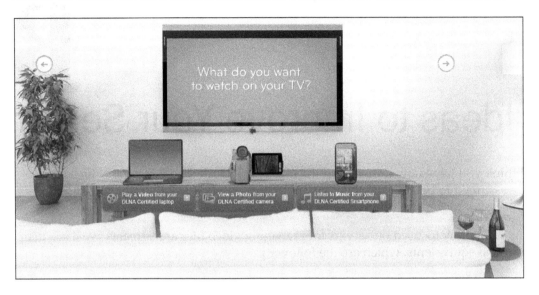

**Digital Living Network Alliance (DLNA)** aims to ease the connection between heterogeneous devices. This means that you can connect with any other DLNA-certified device to share your music, pictures, and videos—regardless of the manufacturer.

# Introducing MiniDLNA

Now that we know what DLNA can do for us, we are going to see how to add it to our existing services. Here comes MiniDLNA.

As defined at `http://sourceforge.net/projects/minidlna/`, this project is as follows:

> *ReadyMedia (formerly known as MiniDLNA) is a simple media server software, with the aim of being fully compliant with DLNA/UPnP-AV clients. It is developed by a NETGEAR employee for the ReadyNAS product line.*

As the Debian packages still use the original name, we will keep calling it MiniDLNA.

# What a DLNA server can do for you

MiniDLNA is able to serve media files such as music (also pictures and videos) to clients on a network that can be applications such as VLC, XBMC, and devices such as portable media players, smartphones, televisions, and gaming systems. You can even connect your Raspberry Pi to it.

# Installing miniDLNA

In order to install miniDLNA, you need to perform the following steps:

1. Install the software:

   ```
   debian@arm:~$ install minidlna
   ```

2. Verify that it's running:

   ```
   debian@arm:~$ /etc/init.d/minidlna status
   ```

```
debian@beaglebone:/var/www$ /etc/init.d/minidlna status
minidlna.service - LSB: Start minidlna at boot time
        Loaded: loaded (/etc/init.d/minidlna)
        Active: active (running) since Sun, 17 Aug 2014 14:55:01 +0000; 4min 54s ago
       Process: 6271 ExecStart=/etc/init.d/minidlna start (code=exited, status=0/SUCCESS)
        CGroup: name=systemd:/system/minidlna.service
                à 6280 /usr/bin/minidlna -f /etc/minidlna.conf -P /run/minidlna/minidlna.pid
```

This is all you need, so you can use the miniDLNA right now.

On Windows Explorer, a BeagleBone device with a MiniDLNA service will appear as follows:

So, you can access the BeagleBone device through miniDLNA as you would do with usual media provider/reader.

# Configuring and customizing miniDLNA

The configuration file is located at:

```
debian@arm:~$ nano /etc/minidlna.conf.
```

This is where you can configure the different options of the server, for example:

- Your share(s):

```
media_dir=/media/usbdrive/Videos
```

- The name that the devices will retrieve:

```
friendly_name=BeagleBoneHomeServer
```

However, if you are still not at ease with the command line, there are additional tools, such as the web interface dedicated to miniDLNA, at http://sourceforge.net/projects/minidlna-web/.

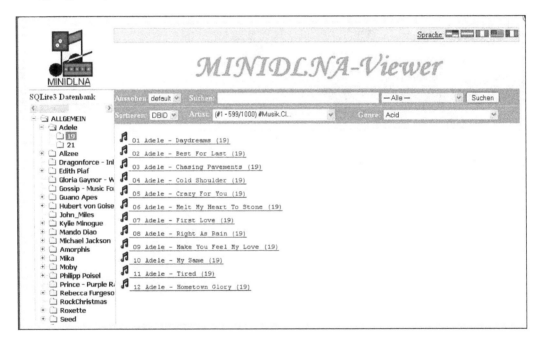

# Subsonic

Here is another server application that is able to support a very large range of clients (for Android, iPhone, Windows Phone, BlackBerry, Roku, Chumby, Sonos, and so on), but the most interesting feature is that a lot of media formats are available as Subsonic support is able to manage on the fly conversions. It is available at `http://www.subsonic.org`, and you will be intrigued by its simplicity; this simplicity doesn't avoid Subsonic to be secure and it can propose different security protocols such as HTTPS/SSL encryption and authentication capability with LDAP or Active Directory (check the documentation for more details).

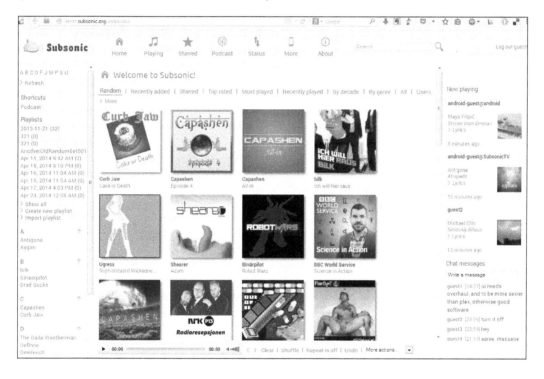

You can access the subsonic online demonstration at `http://demo.subsonic.org/index.view`.

# Installing Subsonic

Like MiniDLNA, Subsonic is really easy to install and simple to configure. Before the installation itself, you need to retrieve a small but needed prerequisite:

```
debian@arm:~$ install openjdk-6-jre
```

Then perform the following steps to install Subsonic:

1.  Click on the **Download** button from the website or directly go to
    `http://www.subsonic.org/pages/download.jsp`.

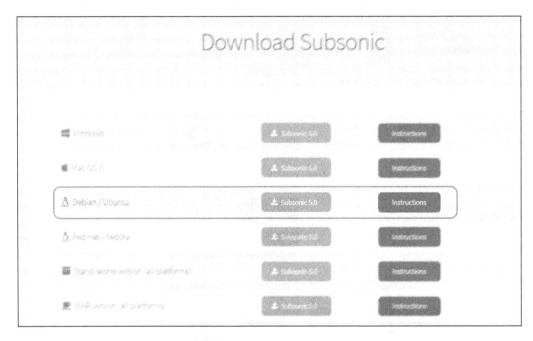

2.  Select the Debian/Ubuntu installer, which will redirect you to the nearest SourceForge site with the latest stable release.

3.  Copy the provided URL and paste it in the BeagleBone command line on PuTTY:

```
debian@arm:~$ Wget http://sourceforge.net/projects/subsonic/files/
subsonic/4.9/subsonic-4.9.deb/download?use_mirror=netcologne -O
subsonic.deb
debian@arm:~$ sudo dpkg -i subsonic.deb
```

# Administering Subsonic

Note that the installer configures your system to start Subsonic automatically when booting. After the installation, open the Subsonic web page at `http://localhost:4040`.

# Changing users

The Subsonic process is run with the root user in the provided default configuration. Therefore, you should the server as a dedicated user with fewer privileges. You can specify these rights by setting the `SUBSONIC_USER` variable in `/etc/default/subsonic`:

```
SUBSONIC_USER=debian
```

Note that nonroot users are by default not allowed to use ports below 1024 then use ports above that. Also, make sure to grant write permissions to the user in the music directories, otherwise changing the album art and tags will fail.

This can be done using the following command:

```
debian@arm:~$ sudo chown debian:debian /var/music
```

The music directory is the one defined in the configuration, as explained in the next section. For more details, check out the documentation at http://www.subsonic. org/pages/getting-started.jsp#1.

# Restarting the service to apply changes

When you modify a configuration, as we did before, consider restarting the service (no need to reboot) so that the changes are applied.

To restart Subsonic, execute the following command:

```
debian@arm:~$ sudo service subsonic restart
```

# Accessing configuration settings

Back to the web view, from **Settings** on the home page, you'll be able to access most of the settings that any network application can propose:

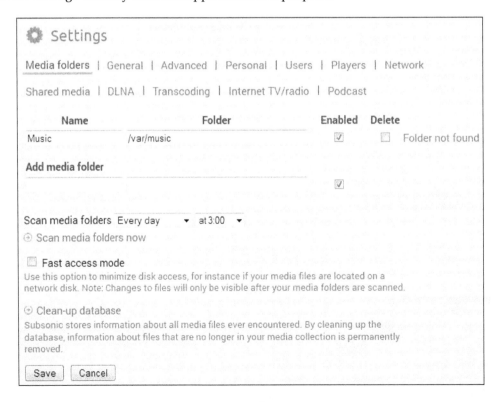

# Advanced configuration

To change the port number, Java memory settings, or other startup parameters, edit the SUBSONIC_ARGS variable in /etc/default/subsonic.

# Troubleshooting

You have all the logs at

```
debian@arm:~$ nano /var/subsonic/subsonic_sh.log
```

This is a good place to look when things are not working as they should.

For example, an issue with a music file might be coming from the transcoder (a software responsible for transforming your files) configuration. Check this in **Setting/players**.

# Index

## S

Savefile_click() function  126
Save_Pattern_click() function  126
Save_To_File(QString Filename)
       function  126
SD card device
  devices, listing with lsblk  85, 86
  dmesg utility, using  86
  investigation, checking  86
  searching  85
security role  46
Setup_gui method  114
software installations  8
Springfield house example
  about  46, 47
  group management  49-51
  groups, applying  51
  role attributions  48
  users, applying  51
  users list, defining  48
Subsonic
  about  137
  administering  139
  advanced configuration  141
  configuration, accessing  140
  installing  138
  online demonstration  137
  restarting, for applying changes  140
  troubleshooting  141
  URL  137
  users, changing  139, 140

## T

Texas Instruments (TI)
  about  89
  developing, with Qt  92
  website  91
TI Linux EZSDK  83
TI Linux unique tools
  benchmarking  90
  cryptos  90
  multimedia  90

power  91
profiling  90
Qt4  90
Qt4/QML  90

## U

upload settings, MediaDrop
  about  30
  file size limit  31
  storage engines  31
users, Springfield house example
  applying  51

## V

VideoLAN menu tab  65
virtualenv  20
virtualenvwrapper  20
Voidrealms
  URL  118

## W

webcam streaming service
  building  57
  drivers and libraries, installing  58
  hardware device, detecting  58
  webcam, detecting  58, 59
  webcam, setting up  60, 61

## Thank you for buying
# BeagleBone Media Center

# About Packt Publishing

Packt, pronounced 'packed', published its first book, *Mastering phpMyAdmin for Effective MySQL Management*, in April 2004, and subsequently continued to specialize in publishing highly focused books on specific technologies and solutions.

Our books and publications share the experiences of your fellow IT professionals in adapting and customizing today's systems, applications, and frameworks. Our solution-based books give you the knowledge and power to customize the software and technologies you're using to get the job done. Packt books are more specific and less general than the IT books you have seen in the past. Our unique business model allows us to bring you more focused information, giving you more of what you need to know, and less of what you don't.

Packt is a modern yet unique publishing company that focuses on producing quality, cutting-edge books for communities of developers, administrators, and newbies alike. For more information, please visit our website at www.packtpub.com.

# About Packt Open Source

In 2010, Packt launched two new brands, Packt Open Source and Packt Enterprise, in order to continue its focus on specialization. This book is part of the Packt Open Source brand, home to books published on software built around open source licenses, and offering information to anybody from advanced developers to budding web designers. The Open Source brand also runs Packt's Open Source Royalty Scheme, by which Packt gives a royalty to each open source project about whose software a book is sold.

# Writing for Packt

We welcome all inquiries from people who are interested in authoring. Book proposals should be sent to author@packtpub.com. If your book idea is still at an early stage and you would like to discuss it first before writing a formal book proposal, then please contact us; one of our commissioning editors will get in touch with you.

We're not just looking for published authors; if you have strong technical skills but no writing experience, our experienced editors can help you develop a writing career, or simply get some additional reward for your expertise.

## Raspberry Pi Media Center

ISBN: 978-1-78216-302-2          Paperback: 108 pages

Transform your Raspberry Pi into a full-blown media center within 24 hours

1.  Discover how you can stream video, music, and photos straight to your TV.

2.  Play existing content from your computer or USB drive.

3.  Watch and record TV via satellite, cable, or terrestrial.

## BeagleBone Home Automation

ISBN: 978-1-78328-573-0          Paperback: 178 pages

Live your sophisticated dream with home automation using BeagleBone

1.  Practical approach to home automation using BeagleBone; starting from the very basics of GPIO control and progressing up to building a complete home automation solution.

2.  Covers the operating principles of a range of useful environment sensors, including their programming and integration to the server application.

3.  Easy-to-follow approach with electronics schematics, wiring diagrams, and controller code all broken down into manageable and easy-to-understand sections.

Please check **www.PacktPub.com** for information on our titles

## Building a Home Security System with BeagleBone

ISBN: 978-1-78355-960-2          Paperback: 120 pages

Build your own high-tech alarm system at a fraction of the cost

1. Build your own state-of-the-art security system.

2. Monitor your system from anywhere you can receive e-mail.

3. Add control of other systems such as sprinklers and gates.

## BeagleBone Robotic Projects

ISBN: 978-1-78355-932-9          Paperback: 244 pages

Create complex and exciting robotic projects with the BeagleBone Black

1. Get to grips with robotic systems.

2. Communicate with your robot and teach it to detect and respond to its environment.

3. Develop walking, rolling, swimming, and flying robots.

www.ingramcontent.com/pod-product-compliance
Lightning Source LLC
Chambersburg PA
CBHW060141060326
40690CB00018B/3945